# The SAS Guide to Teaching

Related titles

*Inside Guide to Training as a Teacher* – Jon Barbuti

*Guerilla Guide to Teaching* – Sue Cowley

*How to Survive your First Year in Teaching* – Sue Cowley

*How to Teach with a Hangover* – Fred Sedgwick

*Sue Cowley's Teaching Clinic* – Sue Cowley

*Teacher's Survival Guide, 2nd Edition* – Angela Thody, Barbara Gray and Derek Bowden

*Trainee Teacher's Survival Guide* – Hazel Bennett

*Ultimate Teacher's Handbook* – Hazel Bennett

# The SAS Guide to Teaching

Brian Carline

continuum

**Continuum International Publishing Group**

The Tower Building          80 Maiden Lane
11 York Road                Suite 704
London                      New York
SE1 7NX                     NY 10038

www.continuumbooks.com

**British Library Cataloguing-in-Publication Data**
A catalogue record for this book is available from the British Library.

ISBN 0–8264–9087–5 (paperback)

**Library of Congress Cataloging-in-Publication Data**
A catalog record for this book is available from the Library of Congress.

Typeset by BC Typesetting Ltd, Bristol BS31 1NZ
Printed and bound in Great Britain by
Antony Rowe Ltd, Chippenham, Wiltshire

For Glynis, whom we all sadly miss.

# Contents

# Acknowledgements

I would like to thank Derek Fawbert, Trevor Hounslow, David Morley, David Summerville and Rob Woodburn for helping me recall some of the amusing anecdotes in the book. Thanks to Helen Aylward for continuing to be the wisest person on the planet.

# Introduction

After 33 years in the teaching profession I do not consider myself to be an expert. I do not know all of the answers. Then again, I have never met anyone who does. However, I've attended many education training courses and been given advice by some individuals who seriously believe they do know it all.

My reasons for writing this book are to share with you many different experiences that have happened to me and some of my teaching colleagues over the last 40 years. I hope that in particular the younger members of the teaching profession will benefit from the advice, guidance and anecdotes. More experienced teaching staff, too, will be reminded of similar things that may have happened to them. Anyone reading this book who has thoughts of possibly joining the world of education will, I trust, also be entertained by gaining some insight into how schools, their staff and students survive on a daily basis.

George Bernard Shaw's shaft of wisdom, 'Those who can, do. Those who cannot, teach', is both outdated and insulting. Were he alive today and to be placed in front of a bottom-band Year 9 class, last period on a windy afternoon, he would instantly retract such an ill-conceived and fatuous remark. Teaching is often viewed as a deadly serious issue. I hope this book will help those sober-minded educationalists to loosen up a little and employ that sense of humour so desperately needed to survive in the job.

I pondered over many possible titles for this book. Contenders such as 'Do we copy this down, Sir?', 'How long to half term?', or 'Has the bell gone yet?' were all possibilities, since they are probably the most frequently asked questions you will hear in your teaching career. I settled on *The SAS Guide To Teaching* because teaching is often perceived by the public as being one of the hardest jobs of all. I recently employed a plumber, who on discovering I was a teacher instantly confirmed that for him to face a class of 30 kids he'd have to be armed with CS-gas canisters, several stun grenades and some very beefy mates. He'd got enough on his plate with his two at home, thank you very much. Mind you, I don't think I could install a central-heating system. Each to their own.

# 1 Raw Beginnings

In August 1971 it suddenly dawned on me that I was in fact unemployed. I had just finished university, where I had taken to student life like John Prescott to a Jaguar. Although I had attempted the minimum-required amount of academic graft, I had experienced more party life than Peter Stringfellow. Consequently, I shared dual billing with a charming Oriental gentleman, Mr Nang, in the third-class honours degree section. Mr Nang's use of syntax was considerably better than that of the average resident of Basildon, but he was slow to copy down meaningful lecture notes. To compound things, he had succumbed to a pernicious, yet ironic, dose of Hong Kong 'flu at the start of his finals. The awards panel settled on an aegrotat of degree class three.

I was uncertain about what to do next. I briefly thought of a sort of gap year until it was pointed out to me that I had just completed three consecutive gap years void of study and direction. I'm not quite sure of how the idea of teaching came to me. I remember waking up one morning and there it was. Factors such as good holidays, unlimited supplies of chalk and awful pay sailed through uncharted waters of my mind. Teacher recruitment in those times allowed you to start the job with no training or experience whatsoever. The graduate-entry mechanism of today gives you a full programme of support and guidance through these virgin times. Nowadays, you should never feel as though you are on your own. In days of yore, new recruits were usually left to sort things out for themselves.

I had hoped the gentleman on the other end of the telephone would have just taken my name and said that should any possibility of a teaching post arise in the next month or so he would give me a ring. I nearly had a cardiac arrest when he gave me the telephone number of a local school with a current vacancy in my subject. As I had the savings balance of a bankrupt I reluctantly contacted the school. The headteacher asked me to bring along all of my academic qualifications, and I made the bold decision to include my cycling proficiency award, together with a certificate indicating that I could swim one length of Salford Municipal Baths. That should really impress him. The complete all-rounder.

The interview with the head took about 15 minutes, mainly discussing George Best's influence at Old Trafford. He was an odd-looking chap with a lumpy face resembling that of a careless beekeeper. He scanned the application form I had hastily completed in the foyer prior to our introduction.

'What class of degree did you get?' he enquired.

'I got a third,' I said in reply. 'But it was a very good third,' I nervously quipped, hoping that this would make light of poor academic accomplishment. I really don't think he cared. He just seemed glad to be fully staffed once more.

I was to assume the full timetable of the current head of department who was on long-term sick leave. I expected the head to say something to the effect of me needing time to prepare for my impending career baptism, but he did not.

'Can you start Monday?' he asked. Today was Friday. I found myself agreeing to this request and left the building with my timetable, A-, O- and CSE-level syllabuses, some scruffy bits of paper and four textbooks.

I had been given a full timetable ranging from upper sixth down to Year 7. It didn't miss a single Year. I don't think I slept at all that weekend. Talk about nervous, I thought I was about to resume bedwetting again after a 16-year period of remission. The head of faculty was supposed to give me support. He was a genial fellow, but unfortunately not too strong in the classroom. I didn't want to copy that teaching style, it would certainly not help me make a success of my new career. Instead I chose to observe as many lessons as my meagre non-contact time would allow, as well as lurk outside classrooms to hear what was happening on the inside. Over the years you will select and reject different ways of communicating information and dealing with situations. This practice helps in shaping your own teaching style and methodology.

For that first year of teaching I barely remained just one lesson ahead of my classes in terms of subject knowledge. I'd never done ecology of a school field with Year 7s before! It all looked like grass to me. Similarly, I had no previous knowledge of the life-cycle of the fungus Phytophthera infestans. My lower-sixth group, however, thought it was a subject on which I was a leading authority. What I didn't know, I would reply with, 'That's something we are going to cover next lesson'. That evening I would spend time researching that question so that I was match-fit for the next session. It is essential that you remain a credible figure with your classes, in terms of subject knowledge as well as classroom control.

I did more work in that first year of teaching than I had ever done in my life. I did make fundamental mistakes. We all do, but we should try not to make those errors again. Your introduction to the job will follow a similar pattern. You will frequently burn the midnight oil to keep pace with the demands of marking. Your lesson-preparation time will consume your weekends. You will start to feel tired and run-down as the terms near their end. You will simply feel there aren't enough hours in the day to complete reports and assess GCSE coursework.

However, despite all of this, there is no better feeling than when pupils tell you they really enjoyed your lesson, or that they felt they really learned something today. Occasionally, you will hear a 'Thanks for that Miss!', or 'Nice one Sir. Mental!' (a term of endearment and congratulation). It's like winning the lottery. It's a feeling that makes you realize it's all worthwhile and that you have made the right career choice.

## 2 Surviving in the Classroom

Richard Dawson was a headteacher in his mid-50s who'd clearly had enough. He'd had to cope with a change from grammar school to comprehensive. He later had to shoulder the responsibilities of local financial management of schools. Both changes were something of a mystery to him. He had been planning to retire early for a number of years, and when he finally received the green light concerning his pension he was off like a whippet chasing a rabbit.

His final term at the school was less than a winding-down process, in fact there appeared to be no 'winding' at all. He could be seen racing the kids out of the school gates at 3.40pm, and frequently appeared in the late book at the start of morning school.

One morning break time he decided to take a short-cut through a school laboratory. He was on his way to see Sid the groundsperson, with whom he would pass many an hour discussing the growing of mammoth leeks. In the lab was a delightful NQT (newly qualified teacher). She was clearing away material she had used in her last lesson and collecting together worksheets for the next. Mr Dawson suddenly strode into the room, giving her quite a shock.

'Good morning, Miss . . . erm? Miss . . . erm? Is everything ok?' he enquired.

'Oh . . . er, yes Mr Dawson. Thank you for asking,' she hastily replied.

'Good. Good. Good', Dawson said indifferently, as he walked past her at great speed. 'Remember, only 40 years to go, Miss . . . erm. Cheerio!' He disappeared in search of his horticultural rendezvous.

Forty years? You'd better make sure you vaguely enjoy your work and can survive in the job. You can afford to make mistakes during your teaching practice. It's not a permanent post and you won't see them again (unless there's a court case).

When you meet a class for the first time, they don't know much about you, and maybe vice versa. The class will want to check you out to see what you're really like. They will want to see if you are soft, easy to manipulate and easy to wind up. In short, they will want to see how much you will let them get away with. In testing you, they will often ask you questions, some of which are quite intrusive:

'Have you got a boyfriend Miss?'

'How old are you Sir?'

'Are you a proper teacher Miss?'

'Where do you live Sir?'

I would be careful not to cooperate with such an inquisition. It's always rather unnerving too when they ask 'Is that your red Mondeo in the car park, Sir?'

In their attempt at sussing you out, the class may be noisy and talk when you are talking. Some of the class may openly chew to test your reaction. Other members of the flock will decide to have an argument with you or each other. You may find you have some itinerants in the group who decide they would like a post-prandial jaunt to see their mate on the other side of the classroom. Many may choose to completely ignore you, with their minds on other things. The remainder may decide to tease and annoy each other by name-calling. Insults of varying degrees will be traded. Pellets or other projectiles are flicked around the room. In total, they may show no intention of cooperating with you, and your lesson plan goes straight out of the window – though not literally, I hope.

If all of the above is happening in front of you, then you are in serious trouble. If all of the above is happening to you in every lesson, then a career change to banking or working on an assembly line at Ford may be the answer.

I think it is wise to state what you require of them *before* they test you. It's best to set out your stall for the year at your initial meeting. Lay down a few ground rules. In the main, students prefer to know where they stand with you – even if it's standing outside the head's door. They also prefer that you are consistent. You have fundamental requirements of them: the core issues relate to talking, movement, presentation of work and safety matters. There are other aspects of behaviour that you will need to raise with them later on. When you get to group work, for example, you will need to clarify the way it should proceed, e.g. respecting other people's points of view, treating others in a way you would like to be treated yourself.

You decide what goes on in your lessons, and so you must make clear right from the start that no one talks while you are talking, and nobody calls out. Rules such as only one person talking at a time, and raising your hand to ask or answer a question succinctly clarify your requirements.

It is most important that you stress there is to be no wandering around the classroom, and they sit where *you* have allowed them to sit. There is no place for nomadic excursions. Some teachers insist that order is created outside the classroom and that students line up in the corridor. This may not be viable in parts of the school where corridors are narrow. You end up with a long single row of pupils that stretches like the thin red line at Balaclava. Instructions have to be passed along the chain and a simple command of 'When you come in, go to your places!' becomes so mutated by Chinese whispers that the last in the queue receives welcome news, 'You can't go in, there are no spaces!'. Nevertheless, if you can assemble them outside the classroom and get them quiet and cooperative, I would certainly endorse this as good practice and a positive start to the lesson.

What has always infuriated me is students fiddling around with things whilst you are talking. It may be rummaging in their bags for a dictionary. This simple act can sound like crushing cardboard boxes in front of you. The worst thing ever is grovelling around to dig out pens from a metal pencil case. The noise it creates is similar to that made by a plumber trying to find a wrench in his tool bag. It is so loud. In simple terms, make 'em keep their hands to themselves.

It is also wise in this introductory session to tell them how you want them to present their work. Clarify the fact that you want them to write in pen and draw in pencil. To ask them to underline headings and draw straight lines using a ruler is not asking for blood. This may come as a bit of a shock to some of the group whose underlining looks as though they are suffering from the after-shocks of Krakatoa. Some students are felt-tip obsessed. It may be because their gran has bought them a bumper pack of 400 from The Pound Shop. I remember when Tipp-Ex first came on the market. It must have been sold to schoolchildren in gallons. It seemed to me that kids enjoyed using the stuff so much, they deliberately made mistakes in their written work so that they could use it. Some kids also used it in large quantities for sniffing. They were the ones who were quite out of it in your lesson and had the tell-tale white bits around their nostrils.

Most important of all is giving the students information about homework. This includes when they are going to be set homework, and when and where to hand it in. Make them log down this information in their planners. They then cannot claim they were not told. However, you know as well as I, there will be some who will.

Some subjects more than others will need to dwell on safety issues in the classroom. PE teachers for example will need to remind their budding athletes not to attempt to catch javelins in mid-air. The technology department will need to reinforce the fact that bongs will no longer be accepted as suitable constructions for a GCSE technology project. This did happen at a school in which I worked. The hashish-crazed Year 11 student painstakingly crafted such a device and passed it off as an oil pourer for salad dishes to his rather innocent teacher. Science teachers will also have to inform students that it is highly dangerous practice to put drops of nitric acid on the seats of classmates. Recipients finish up with not only sore, but burnt and enlarged anal sphincters.

In the physics departments of schools there is a piece of equipment called Fletcher's Trolley. It is a flat sheet of wood with two sets of wheels underneath. Its use is in mechanics in GCSE physics to demonstrate velocity and acceleration principles. In a school in north London I saw them being used inventively as skateboards along the science department corridor.

IT equipment needs a mention here. Nowadays the majority of classrooms are equipped with such hardware. It certainly does take a hammering from our computer-literate students. I feel the term hammering is a suitable one. I have seen students thumping the keys as if they were using a 1920s Remington typewriter. A former colleague of mine told me that when someone set off fart spray in his lesson, the kids all picked up the keyboards and started to waft them up and down to ventilate the room. That's one use of Windows for supplying fresh air, if you'll pardon the pun. As for mouse balls, I've never seen so many emasculated specimens.

Some teachers can project their voices with ease. You have to keep in mind that you must be audible even to the lively lot on the back row. There is a place for raising your voice to a shout, but this will only have a salutary effect on special occasions. It is a technique best held in reserve.

I once had an office immediately below a young teacher who was shouting from the moment his class entered the room until the time they left. His classes were always noisy, with him being the chief culprit. When someone in the class did something that was worthy of a verbal rocket the guy burned out his vocal cords. In terms of volume he simply had nowhere to go. Be careful of the pitch and tone of your voice. The last thing you must do is to either precipitate or antagonize conflict situations.

If you are the archetypal 'nice person' you must not make the fatal, often career-ending mistake, of being too friendly with a class. Even if you personally were taught by Pol Pot and are anxious to redress the humanitarian balance, you must not commit such a cardinal sin. If you do, they will take liberties and see you as a soft touch. Letting your true personality come through with a class takes a long time. First you must affirm leadership, credibility and respect. If your class calls you Dave and drinks your coffee, then you've made a few mistakes.

I am always reminded of the theatre when I am asked about good classroom practice. You should never lose eye contact with your class for long periods of time. Actors who tread the boards learn the golden rule: 'Never turn your back on your audience, luvvie'. It's the same law for the classroom. If you are writing on the board for long periods of time, you don't know what's going on behind you. You soon find out when there's a sudden scream of pain. While you've been drawing a beautiful graph of the yearly rainfall in Fort William, poor old Winston Quigley's blazer has been set on fire by his schizoid mate. All hell then breaks loose.

On some occasions it may be wise to part company with a student who either has, or is about to cause, a major behavioural problem. The school or the department in which you work should have a policy on this. I would suggest it is unhelpful simply to cast some recalcitrant into the corridor. This can create more problems than it solves. I have seen some instances when teachers finish up with more youngsters in the corridor than in the classroom. One such group then decided to have a game of five-a-side in the neighbouring playground.

Schools often have a 'time out' policy to assist certain individuals to cool off in tense and potentially troublesome situations. These should be used sparingly and wisely. Most departments have a mutual-support policy whereby other members of staff can help you out on an occasional basis by providing temporary homes for non-cooperatives. Putting such a malefactor at the back of someone's sixth-form group is a good remedy – unless the offender is a member of the sixth form. Work out with your head of department any possible strategies, and have a copy of their timetable so you know where you can find them. If there is an arrangement, then make sure the student has work to do, otherwise you will not be too popular. Remember you will be disrupting their lesson, and if there is no work for the student to do then this will only compound the problem.

Schools have a senior member of staff 'on call' roster. All I would say on that one is that it is meant for emergency situations only. Use it, and don't abuse it. Schools that are perceived as being successful in their management of student behaviour are so because the establishment has created a mutually supportive culture, which stems from the top and permeates through all areas of the school. Even the lunchtime supervisors do not feel they are on their own.

Much is spoken these days about body language and the way it can influence situations. Be careful about certain aspects of your body language with students. Standing face to face with a student will cause an immediate deterioration of a situation. Safeguarding someone's personal space is important. Be careful about eye contact too, it can sometimes provoke conflict or threaten. I once worked with a senior member of staff whose customer relations were appalling. Whether it be teacher, parent or pupil, he was in their face throughout their encounter. As they would take a few steps back, he would advance a few steps forward. It was dialogue on the move and an experience people found most intimidating.

If you have a sense of humour in teaching it can help you through the day. If you haven't got a sense of humour, then I'd go out and buy one as soon as possible. It is a pre-requisite for the job. However, I have worked with a small number of colleagues who employ rather hurtful sarcasm in their dealings with students. It is an unacceptable strategy and I would advise similar practitioners to keep their sarcastic and often humiliating remarks to themselves. The majority of youngsters cannot deal with such acerbity and they often feel degraded.

It is very often difficult to keep yourself from laughing out loud at some of the things kids say, particularly if they are deadly serious about something. I was once teaching a lesson on floating and sinking to a middle-band Year 9 class. I was trying to lead them into thinking about everyday applications of the simple theory we had just discussed. I asked the question, 'Can anyone tell me the name of the line on the side of a ship? It tells the captain exactly how much cargo he/she can load onto the ship without it sinking whilst sailing the seas.' (I was searching for the Plimsoll line, for non-physicists.)

There was a short silence as the gearwheels started to turn, and eventually a hand shot up from the depths.

'Is it P & O Stena line sir?' enquired the deadly serious girl.

When you hear a corker like that you are tempted to burst into laughter with the rest of the class. I did find it difficult to maintain my composure, but I am glad to say, I managed it. The skill was now to stop the class giggling and making comments. It was important to restore the now fragile dignity of the girl.

'Don't worry Lisa,' I said. 'It was the clumsy way I asked the question. A lot of ships do have that painted on their sides Lisa, I know. That was a genuine mistake to make. It is a line near that. Good effort anyway, Lisa. It shows you are thinking. Well done!'

The class chuckles subsided and the girl felt better. Mission accomplished.

Kids are usually deadly serious with their answers to your questions. The knack is not to say a direct no to their incorrect answers but to let them down gently. It is important to maintain their interest and motivation. So, if someone answers the question,

'What do we mean by the expression a terminal illness?'

'Someone getting sick at an airport, Sir?' Your response should be,

'Not quite, Wayne. I know how you got that answer and many people would think that. But I have to say not quite, but nearly, to that one mate. Good answer and well done anyway.' You quickly move to the next hand that is raised. The important thing is not to wet yourself with laughter.

You will have many bad days in your teaching career. By that I mean when things don't seem to go your way. It may start with your journey to school and the Accrington gyratory traffic system failing to gyrate. It may start even earlier than that if you have a row with your partner, or your baby girl is sick all down your suit just before you leave the house. To compound things, you may find you lose your only free period of the day and discover it's the worst class in the school that you've been given. You may also be on duty at break time, meaning a cold cup of coffee or nothing at all. This accumulation of negatives may put you in a bad mood. It is important to remember that at times like these you must not lose control with the classes or people you teach. You may be a skilled classroom practitioner under normal circumstances, but this dreadful day you are having may tempt you to react or respond irrationally to testing situations. Don't knee-jerk react to a sudden stimulus, and remember to calm yourself before calming the child. It may be that Mercedes Wilkinson has just blown the biggest ever chewing gum bubble that totally destroys the pace and challenge of your lesson. That is no reason to go over and garrotte her. It is always wise to stop and think for a moment before you remedy a situation, or before you garrotte her. This is particularly important when you are having a bad day. I always thought of my pension . . . and also of the possible headlines in the local newspaper.

Once I had to employ all of my professional human resources skills to bail out a member of staff who was having a bad day. It was last period on a cold and windy February afternoon and he was teaching a rather unpleasant Year 11 group. A brief summary of the event is that a student who had not been paying attention to instructions in the practical lesson destroyed the wrong piece of plastic by sawing it into pieces. The large sheet was meant for the teacher to use with another group the next day. The irate teacher, discovering that his lesson with an equally challenging group had now dissolved before his eyes, exploded and called the student a name equivalent to a copulating anus (it won't take long for you to work that one out). The outburst consumed a lot of my time in resolving matters with the student and his parents. The teacher was appreciative of the school maintaining his employment and allowing him to complete his 40 years.

The thing you must not do with kids is to get involved in an argument with them. They enjoy confrontation, and the majority of them are better at arguing than we are. Allowing situations like this to develop will often lead to you losing face with the group. Try to avoid audiences because if an argument or a conflict should start with a student then you will lose credibility in front of the group. Kids who are successful in drawing you into an argument gain strength from their mates. They will play to the gallery better than Peter Kay. It is much easier to speak with the miscreant on their own rather than fall into their argument trap.

As head of house, I once had dealings with a recidivist who was most talented at winding up members of staff.

His skills would be employed on kitchen staff and up as far as the head. He loved an audience and his confidence increased the bigger the crowd. He was a well-built lad and something of a bully. Some of the students would say that if George said the word shit, you did! However, if you removed him from his pool of sycophants he became a different person. Just as Sampson lost his strength after being given a short back and sides by Delilah, so George's will to win would ebb away. So remember, on many occasions it's much easier to speak with someone on their own and away from the group, in order to get the result you want.

Avoid public challenges or proclamations that really can't come to fruition. Exclamations like 'If you do that again, I'll have you out of this group forever!'

Sure as eggs, the individual will do it again and you will find that you cannot banish the child forever. When you threaten the impossible you have to back down, and you lose credibility and respect. Your pupils have good memories, and if the youngster who was previously heading your expulsion list is still there, then it doesn't look too good.

When you use corrective disciplining, plan your language of discipline. Try to balance this with some words of encouragement. Comments such as: 'Why don't you keep your big fat mouth shut Higginbottom?' are most unhelpful. You will be sinking to his level. I can understand why you made such a request. It's probably because that specimen has been interrupting your lesson from the first minute. Nerves, frustration, tiredness and an adrenaline rush have caused your outburst. It's rather difficult on occasions to say, 'Hold on Darren! What's the matter with you today? You're slowing us all down. Come on mate, you can do better than that. Sort it out, will you?'

It may work, and will, if the rest of the group get fed up with him. However, you will often deal with students for whom there is no cure.

When you apply consequences for common rule-breaking behaviours, emphasize the certainty of the consequences rather than the severity. Establish a sense of fairness and even-handedness in your actions. It is generally accepted that the teachers' code should be 'firm but fair'. Remember also to separate the behaviour from the student. Kids are very sharp at picking you up on this if you do not.

It is very easy to be drawn by students into issues which spring from the initial cause for concern. If you allow this to happen you will become sidetracked and you will lose valuable time and control. Some students, particularly those who are seen to be habitually challenging, are very good at this sort of thing. A quick request to cease chatter can sometimes be allowed to drift into seemingly irrelevant issues if you're not careful. A suitable example could be if a student has a CD player out on their table. Your request for them to put it away in their bag could lead to a mega conflict. The student may well come back with, 'But I ain't listening to it!' This reply could be offering you an argument if you want one. Stick to your guns and say, 'I know you're not Astrid, I didn't say you were. Just put it in your bag please.'

They may often be tempted to come back again with further information to lengthen the dispute. Again, don't be drawn, keep to the original request. If you've covered areas like these in your initial encounters, you can always remind them of these classroom basics. Some youngsters will spoil for an argument. Don't give them one.

Some days will go well for you and others not so well. Students will attempt to wind you up, and some will succeed. I think it's worth remembering that it's all in a day's work for them and they've usually forgotten about any verbal clashes at the end of the day. Your mission is to emerge from your lessons with your nervous system and dignity intact, as well as making your teaching points. Don't worry if you have to jettison some or all of your lesson plan to maintain control. Every teacher has to do this at some stage in their teaching career.

I had been teaching for ten years and thought myself to be fairly competent. In my new school I was given a Year 8 class who were deemed unteachable. In my early encounters with them I would say they were out of control. It was a class of 32 pupils. There were five highly volatile EBD (emotionally and behaviourally disturbed) kids. Another 16 were regularly visited by the educational psychologist and attended Child Guidance. The remaining bunch seemed as temperamentally fragile as the rest. I had them three times a week, each session being 1 hour 25 minutes long. I lived in fear of that class for a full school year. They would dominate my life. I would wake up the night before I taught them in cold sweats. They would even be with me at weekends. It took me nearly two terms to tame them and keep them under some control. To maintain order and keep them in their seats I got them to copy worksheets and answer questions. There was very little classroom teaching, and I suppose very little learning, but it kept the majority of them occupied. I prayed for truancies. It's always the same, those you don't want to be there are the regular attenders.

After about a term and a half of this we made a little progress and I allowed some practical sessions to take place. Towards the end of the year some of them actually said they liked science. There were days when I felt like giving up, but I'm glad I persevered. They were the biggest bunch of disturbed kids I've ever taught as a class. Don't worry if you are having similar experiences. It's not just you. If you haven't experienced nightmare groups in your career then you've been extremely fortunate or you've been teaching in the private sector.

You are learning your trade all the time. If you make mistakes, and you will make plenty, don't get too down about it. Learn from them. You certainly won't make those errors again. Remember, teaching is one of the hardest jobs to do on this planet. To do it well requires many skills and talents. When you begin your teaching career you will slowly become more adroit. Learning some of these skills, however, will require more time and effort than others. All schools possess some excellent classroom practitioners. You will know who they are and the kids will certainly identify them for you. Ask to see these people in action so that you can see how they deal with certain issues. Your teaching life will be about learning from others, and often teachers are a curious mixture of techniques, styles and delivery that they've seen work successfully with other colleagues. There's nothing wrong with that at all, as long as the end product works.

Children have their own ideas about the qualities of good teachers. There does seem to be a general agreement that they are the ones who explain things clearly. They are strict but not too authoritarian. Kids don't like teachers who are too trendy or permissive. They like to know where they stand and that you treat them as individuals. The firm-but-fair code comes in here. They like it if you are consistent and fair in the use of rewards and punishments. If you are boring they'll soon give you the message. They prefer it if you are interesting and provide them with a variety of stimulating work. They like you to have a sense of humour but not be sarcastic. (Wragg *et al.*, *Class Management in the Secondary School*, RoutledgeFalmer 2000)

## To summarize:

1. Set out your stall for the year in your first lesson, and establish core routines. The students know where they stand if you do this. These should include:
   - If possible, get the class ready outside the classroom.
   - When they come in, you decide where they sit.
   - Tell them to sit down, settle them and then call the register.
   - Don't talk over their noise.
   - Cover your requirements from the class such as:
     a) Hands up to answer/ask questions, and no calling out.
     b) No talking when the teacher is talking.
     c) No fidgeting around with pencil cases, bags or books whilst the teacher is talking.
     d) Write in pen/diagrams in pencil/use of rulers.
     e) Homework requirements – days it will be set, where and when it is to be handed in.
     f) No wandering around the room.

g) To have a respect for other people's views and opinions.
2. Avoid confrontations or arguments with students.
3. Don't be drawn into side issues and don't allow any challenges to escalate.
4. Tackle certain situations on a one-to-one basis.
5. Don't always shout – there's a time and a place for raising your voice.
6. Don't threaten things you can't deliver.
7. Be careful how you use humour. Never humiliate a child, and avoid sarcasm.
8. Avoid persistent criticism of a child.
9. Seek help if you need it from your head of department or other department members. It is best to have a pre-arranged formula for this. You may have to use the senior member of staff who is 'on call'.
10. Try not to lose control, and try to take the heat out of potentially unpleasant situations.
11. Observe other teachers and pick out the good bits of their classroom management and practice.
12. Don't be too friendly at first, slowly allow your true personality to come through after you've established a good, positive relationship with the group.
13. The perceived negatives of corrective disciplining of a student should be balanced with positive words of encouragement.
14. Forget your personal feelings about individual students. It is important to separate this from their

behaviour. This will avoid instances of 'You're picking on me!'

15. Be consistent when tackling behavioural issues, and emphasize the certainty of the consequences of their behaviour.

16. Maintain your dignity and leadership role in the classroom.

17. Remember, some students enjoy trying to antagonize teachers. It's all in a day's work for them. They don't take it home with them, so after you've done your preparation at home for the next school day, switch off and concentrate on other things. Enjoy yourself.

18. Also remember the good days outnumber the bad. That's the theory, anyway!

# 3 Dealing with Parents

If you had a happy childhood with two parents who remained together in matrimonial bliss throughout your teenage years, you were extremely fortunate. It's one common mistake made by some new teaching recruits that they expect the youngsters they now deal with on a daily basis to have had the same uncomplicated youth as themselves.

What we must understand is that the term 'family' is simply what we find when we knock on their door. The traditional textbook norm of two parents, two children under 16, father going out to work and mother at home amounts to about five per cent of the population. The real norm is the other 95 per cent that contains all kinds of possibilities. Throw into the arena statistics like nearly one third of all marriages end in divorce, and that at any given time nearly one quarter of all children of school age (regardless of social and geographical background) are involved in some process of marital breakdown or divorce, then you will see what many of the kids we teach have to endure even before they set foot in the school.

You may have studied a subject to degree level and entered the teaching profession to make this subject come alive in the minds of youngsters. You must remember that you will sooner or later come into contact with the parents or carers of these children. The nature of these families can often come as a bit of a shock to you. As a form tutor your job is to really get to know the pupils in your charge, and as this learning process takes place you will engage with their parents. You will learn that some can be pushy parents. Teachers very often say of themselves that they as parents are classic examples. You may come across obsessive or over-anxious parents. Some parents cannot cope with adolescence and the associated issues which affect their sons and daughters. Some families cannot shoulder the daily demands of life, and the children in these families become the casualties of this breakdown.

You will come across youngsters who have had to cope with periods of prolonged illness of a family member, or kids who have lost one or even both of their parents. It may be this loss is due to bereavement, separation or divorce. Some families suffer incredible financial hardship. One or both parents may be unemployed and yet they still strive to keep up with other families. Finally, you may deal with families in which there has been child abuse. One or more of the siblings may have been subjected to neglect, physical, emotional or even sexual abuse.

When you start out in teaching, your first introduction to parents is usually parents' evenings, or nowadays as a tutor in an ARD (Academic Review Day). The majority of these parents' evenings now take place immediately after school. In the olden days, 6.30pm to 9.30pm was the usual slot. Some would start as late as 7.30pm. When I worked in London, several of the younger teachers, plus a couple of alcohol-dependent die-hard 50 year olds, would go out for a few pints beforehand. I never thought it wise to spend the consultation evening breathing best bitter over concerned parents. It didn't do your teacher cred much good. Nor did it look good when you had to leave the hall for the fifth time in the evening to evacuate your bladder. Some staff would visit The Kohinoor just off the Balls Pond Road for a pre-meeting curry. One celebrated young man could consume a lamb bhuna starter followed by a chicken vindaloo with garlic naan, and then proceed to finish off all the platter residues on the table. He would hold court with his parents smelling like the Nawab of Lahore. It is also inadvisable to feast on such rich food in case you develop an acute attack of the Bengal Trots. Your comments about possible GCSE grades may be all too brief as you disappear out of the hall to remedy your problem. Kebabs of all descriptions can also cause you to effuse noxious fumes that may be rather over-powering for parents.

You may find that some of these consultation evenings are arranged rather early in the year. This may prove to be a problem, particularly if you have many lower school classes (Years 7, 8 and 9) on your timetable. They are usually large classes and it's often impossible to learn all of the kids' names in such a short span of time. You may start to talk to a parent about a particular student and suddenly realize half way through your con-versation that you're talking about the wrong person. Drastic action is then called for to save the situation. One such dialogue could be:

PARENT: 'Are you saying she's inattentive? All of the other teachers we've seen tonight have said how quiet and well behaved she is.'

TEACHER (who is half way along the road to Damascus, suddenly gets the message that he's talking about the girl who sits in the row immediately behind her): 'Er, you, you, you are quite right. She is. She is atten-tive . . . er, but she did have an unsettled start. But, I am now pleased to say. Yes, very pleased to say that she is coping well with the work and making good progress. Yes, no complaints!'

PARENT (with a slightly confused look on her face): 'Oh, well, er . . . I'll have to speak to her about that poor start Mr Harris.'

TEACHER (now anxious that things be smoothed over and as a desperate attempt to rescue his credibility): 'Ooh, that was in the past Mrs Cooper. She has picked up really well and I wouldn't want you to upset her new-found appetite for the subject. I'd leave well alone Mrs Cooper and just say how pleased I am with her progress.'

It is also possible to make a faux pas with gender. I have been guilty of speaking about a pupil using the pronoun he instead of she. I was caught out because of poor timetabling, having been given three Year 7 classes, all with large numbers of students. A couple of parents introduced themselves as Mr and Mrs Duffy, the parents of Terry. I really didn't have a clue about whom they were enquiring. Because the name was not known to me as a class psychopath or lesson disrupter, I felt I'd be on a good wicket if I used non-specific terms such as 'he made a satisfactory start in the subject' and 'he is making good progress'. I was just about to embark on another pleasantry when Dad cut in and reminded me Terry was, in fact, a girl. I visibly flushed with embarrassment and blamed my pre-senile dementia. I did feel an absolute noodle.

It's very often the case that at parents' evenings you never end up seeing the parents of the pupils you really need to see. By this, I mean the pupils who never do their homework or are a royal pain in the derrière in lessons.

Nowadays it is common for pupils to accompany their mums and dads to these consultation sessions. It's fun to look at parents and offspring to see where Darren inherits his ugly looks or obnoxiousness. A mate of mine, when faced with eccentric or odd-looking parents, would often try to imagine them at the moment they conceived young Debbie to make the time pass more entertainingly.

At these brief information exchanges, always remember to be polite and courteous. Stand up and shake hands with them. Remember, you may have many parents to see and so you must be concise. You may only be able to speak with them for five minutes, but it's amazing what you can pack into that short period of time. Don't get drawn into any side issues, there's simply not the time. Parents want to know how their children are coping with the work. They want to know if they are behaving themselves in class, they want to know about homework. They also want some idea about how they are relative to other class members, e.g. are they about middle for the group, etc. Parents who want to support the work done in class will want to know if there's anything they can do to help.

Having students in GCSE classes will mean their parents will want some idea as to examination prognosis. I would tread very cautiously here because some parents may revisit your earlier forecasted grade and want to know why you or the school has not informed them of a sudden change for the worse towards the end of Year 11. It may be wise to give non-specific grade predictions such as 'achieve a reasonable grade if he/she maintains their efforts'.

Markbooks and planners with their class registers can be a useful asset. They can illustrate praise of student performance and can also be an ally to highlight lack of homework, or even poor attendance. Some highly organized staff take piles of exercise books to the meeting. I still cannot understand the practice to this day. I've seen staff with three sets of books stacked around them like blocks of high-rise flats. If ever I did take exercise books down with me for parents to scrutinize, it was only those that needed serious remedial attention.

Don't get too bogged down with chit-chat or you'll find yourself still sat there at 10pm with five sets of parents still lurking around. Caretaking staff will start stacking tables and asking you to lift your feet up whilst they sweep around you to prepare the hall for tomorrow's assembly. Above all, don't get into any arguments with parents at these sessions. If the meeting appears to be turning acrimonious and you feel threatened or intimidated by the parent, then summon help from a colleague, or draw the conversation immediately to a close.

I attended one Year 9 evening many years ago, when a fellow worker who was regarded as being as stable as sweating gelignite suddenly stood up and started shouting at his visiting parent. The parent kept his cool and sat there listening to the tirade of adjectives and arm-waving from the capricious educator who was then unceremoniously removed from the hall by a large, no-nonsense deputy head and a somewhat ashen-faced head. To make matters worse, the scuffle continued quite noticeably behind the curtains on the school stage. The chap taught a shortage subject and had only been employed on a temporary contract. It was hoped his mania would not surface for two terms. The gamble sadly had not paid off.

As you journey through your career you will become more skilled at keeping your meetings to the allotted time. Statements such as, 'So, that's really a summary of her progress and performance and I look forward to meeting you again next year', are used to indicate a termination of the meeting. Ensure the last three words of the sentence are said while you are rising from your seat with an outstretched hand.

In your role as a form tutor you will have to attend meetings with parents because some problem has arisen. Parents may ask to see you, or invariably you will ask to see them. In certain pastoral matters that require attention, your head of year/house or head of school section may take the reins. They may also ask you to be present. Often, if they feel it's a relatively straight-forward matter, they'll ask you to represent the school since as the tutor you are supposed to have greatest knowledge of the pupil. However, if ever you feel you lack confidence in your own ability to handle such a meeting, seek assistance. Never be put in a position where you feel you are vulnerable.

There are some golden rules which you should follow when attending parents' meetings. Many parents have unhappy memories of their own schooling and they may feel uncomfortable about even being in the school building and having to speak with teachers. When you meet them you should make them feel welcome, shake their hand and take them along to an office or empty classroom where you will be able to talk in private. Do not see them in a public place like a foyer, the corridor or hall. You never know what personal issues they may divulge in the meeting. Make sure it's somewhere where you both can speak freely and not be overheard. However, always know where you can summon assistance if you need it.

I was once given an office as head of upper school that was constructed of plasterboard and backed onto the boys' toilets. The room was given me by a former grammar school head who didn't really understand pastoral work and what it entailed. Consequently, I refused to see parents in this flimsy shell after I got fed up with my conversations being punctuated by the rectal philharmonics of the adjoining occupants. Some privacy!

I have known parents to go for a few pints before coming into the school as a personal confidence-boosting exercise. One parent, a former Jamaican resident, positively reeked of ganja. One essential skill for dealing with people is to listen to what they say, and make sure you *understand* what they are saying. Some parents go around the houses before reaching the relevant issue. Some parents find it difficult to articulate their thoughts and wishes. They may have language difficulties. One such example was when I had to invite to the school the parents of a Year 9 Greek pupil who had systematically liberated about 20 calculators from his classmates. He had established a lucrative business selling them on to pupils in the year above. The boy's father and older sister arrived with him. His sister was there to translate for the dad whose English was none-too good. I explained to the sister what the boy had done and she dutifully translated to Dad. As the translation process ensued I could see the father getting more and more agitated. Eventually he stood up and started making a strange sawing gesture against his fingers. I hastily asked the sister what this meant. She too was now verging on hysteria. 'He's going to cut off his fingers!' she yelled. Apparently there was an unwritten ruling in the remote island settlement where the family had originated, that anyone found stealing from their neighbours would lose a number of fingers commensurate with the crime. I quickly explained to the dad that the school would punish Theo and that there was no need to implement local byelaws. It took a few minutes for him to regain his composure. The boy too was in need of a change of underwear. Eventually everyone calmed down and we all parted on good terms, and each with the correct number of digits.

A similar instance happened to a fellow Year head when he was seeing a parent of a 14-year-old boy who was being quite rude and objectionable to his teachers. The parent took on board all my colleague said and was profusely apologetic about his son's behaviour. The parent then stood up and proceeded to unbuckle his large leather belt. Then he proclaimed he was now going to teach the boy acceptable behaviour by beating him senseless with the aforementioned article. Needless to say my colleague prevented such an episode, much to the relief of the terrified youth.

Sometimes when you have a meeting with parents about a matter with which they are unhappy, the parent will come in fired up and ready for battle. I find it is best to let them have their say and for their bellicose manner to slowly burn itself out. Usually parents cannot maintain a lengthy adrenaline rush and once they have been allowed to say what they have to say, they feel better. Often they finish up agreeing with you. Parents may say harsh or inaccurate things. They may be losing their temper, but on no account should you lose yours. Heavy meetings like this will mean you should be accompanied by a senior member of staff who will be skilled in dealing with meetings of this nature. Sometimes the body language of parents will indicate there's trouble on the horizon. They may point towards you or gesticulate. Some may shout and remonstrate. Some may even get out of their seat. The best prescription in cases like these is to remain calm and courteous and be careful of your own body language. Don't you lose your temper even though you might feel a short sentence, ending with the word off, is what the antagonist needs. In certain cases it's often wise to bring the meeting to a rapid close if the parent remains openly hostile and is refusing to listen to your cogent account.

It's also wise to see the parents separately from the student before you see both parent and student together. When you see parents who are divorced or separated, be careful not to take sides or apportion blame in these tug-of-love situations.

Always make interview notes. If there are two of you then it's a lot easier with one of you acting as scribe. Some heads of year often read back to parents the summary notes of the meeting, which can be particularly useful when an action plan has been agreed upon. Keep these notes on file. Sometimes in meetings you will have to read witness statements or other pieces of important paperwork, so make sure you are fully prepared. Ensure these statements are dated and signed and have them at hand. It is important that you present parents with facts and not opinions.

Because incidents very often involve other students it is most important that you do not let parents have access to these youngsters. You may meet parents who will demand such an encounter, but stick to your guns, this must not be allowed to happen.

In certain instances be prepared to make a compromise over certain issues. For example, in school-refusal cases don't always demand an instant return to a full timetable, slowly try to phase the youngster back into school. This may be a rather protracted process, but it can improve the situation.

Meetings can drag on and there's a danger if it's an after-school meeting of it encroaching into your bedtime. Always allot a certain length of time for this meeting – half an hour tops! Draw the meeting to a close with a well-tried concluding statement like: 'Well, thanks for coming up to the school to discuss this matter, I feel we've covered all of the important areas . . .'

I recall one inebriated parent entering the school brandishing a baseball bat, claiming he didn't have any appointment to see any teacher but he was going to knock seven shades of faeces out of the headteacher. I momentarily thought this might be a good idea, since the majority of staff disliked the chap. However, loyalty got the better of me as I joined two other terrified teachers in overpowering this man to save my gallant leader's cranium. We spent the next 20 minutes sat on top of the would-be assailant in the school secretary's office, waiting for the police to arrive.

I was having a drink in a pub a few years ago and I happened to overhear a young and rather self-opinionated member of the public talking about the amount of income tax she was paying. I was tempted to join in the conversation and support her vendetta towards the Inland Revenue when she suddenly started barking on about vast sums of money from this income tax being given to the DSS. 'There's no such thing as poverty anymore,' was part of her diatribe. I didn't leap in and say my two penneth, although I was very much tempted. I finished my drink and left the young lady with her audience. My reason for recalling this person's observations is that just because many of us lead relatively comfortable lives, we must not assume that poverty and deprivation rarely exist in our society. Many of the youngsters we teach come from family structures where indigence and hardship prevail.

From time to time I did home-visits to parents when the need arose. I was often accompanied by an EWO (Education Welfare Officer). In inner London this valuable workforce were often called Education Social Workers. As a pastoral middle manager they were a group of people who helped you do your job more effectively. The only problem was that there was always a shortage of them and as soon as you developed a good working relationship with one, they moved on. They would be of help in sorting out issues from student attendance to arranging work permits for youngsters. They were of immense value too in dealing with issues that directly stemmed from poverty. Many of my colleagues will agree that there is still tremendous deprivation and poverty out there. Visit the homes of some students and you see at first hand the hardship that they and their families have to endure.

I accompanied my EWO to do a home-visit to a family whose son was in my year. The boy was refusing to come to school because, as we eventually discovered, he was being bullied by members of his form. The boy did smell and his rather cruel classmates teased him about this. His parents were not on the telephone and the only way we could contact the family was via letter. We received no replies from this mail, recorded or otherwise. The EWO thus arranged a home-visit after briefly calling on them one morning. I had read this young man's file when he entered my charge. It made depressing reading. Dad was out of work and had been for some time. He was suffering from manic depressive psychosis and his prolonged bouts of melancholia and painful introspection made him a difficult person to be with in the family unit. Mum tried her hardest to keep the family buoyant. There were five children in the family of various ages. Mum depended upon Jason to run errands and to look after the kids when she did her cleaning jobs. The family really did find it difficult to cope with the daily challenges of life. Jason smelt because washing his shirts and underwear was done on an ad hoc basis or not at all. 'Ad hoc ad astra' would have been on their family crest. The visit to their home was a real shocker to me and Sheila, the EWO. We were alarmed at what we saw. I had not anticipated such untidiness, chaos and deprivation. We did get some help for the family. We did get Jason back into school. His cleanliness did improve for some time and the intimidation eventually subsided. The things we achieved only put an Elastoplast on a running sore.

You learn to expect anything when you're in teaching. How could a dad walk out on his family the night before his daughter is about to take her first GCSE examination? How can a parent refuse to accept that their daughter is having an adverse effect on the progress of other students in lessons? How can they then accuse the school of picking on their daughter when all of her teachers cite examples of truculence and disruptive behaviour? And so it goes . . .

One final thought about contacting parents. Some prove extremely elusive. Some may refuse to contact the school despite numerous requests by post and even registered mail. There was one particular dad we used to call the Scarlet Pimpernel, he was so evasive.

If ever there's a difficulty catching parents in, telephone them during *Coronation Street* or *EastEnders*, you're sure to nab one then.

Towards the end of my teaching career I was proud of establishing an active group of parents who worked with a small number of teachers to tackle issues like parents as co-educators, Internet protection for children and safer journeys to school, etc. We would meet each half term. The meetings were always enjoyable and good spirited. It was at one such gathering in the summer term that a parent put me in a position that demanded all of my public speaking skills and personal control.

I had just started the meeting and was in the process of trawling through the minutes of our last session when a parent entered the room looking rather flustered and full of sincere apologies about her tardiness. I smiled pleasantly and nodded but continued with my discourse. Approximately two minutes after this, the same parent emitted the loudest and longest shaft of flatulence I have ever heard. It veritably rattled the windows. I couldn't believe my own ears. There was no apology, which in retrospect might have made things worse. What should I do? The male in me wanted to burst out laughing but as leader of this happy band I must show some decorum. I decided to keep my head low, mainly to avoid eye contact with the head of Year 10 who was seated immediately opposite. I was doing well. I was keeping to the agenda with no sign of repetition or deviation. I could sense that I was as red as a ripe tomato and my heart was racing. I was continuing to address the group and I knew I would come through this one. Out of the corner of my eye I noticed the head of Year 11 with head bowed as though he was in prayer, but his shoulders were bouncing up and down at the rate of two per second. He was, indeed, finding it extremely difficult to repress his laughter. He was a giggler at the best of times but this sudden and unanticipated rasping barrage of flatus had sent him beyond control. He eventually pulled out a handkerchief and smothered his face with it, stood up and proclaimed the words 'Nose bleed!' and left the room. Not one parent ever referred to this colonic episode. The staff, however, were uncontrollable at morning break as the head of Year 11 made mention of the event.

## To summarize:

1. At parent/teacher consultation sessions.

   - Make the parents feel welcome, stand up and shake hands.
   - Make sure you can put pupil faces to names. Make notes in your markbook or seating plan when you call the subject register in lessons prior to the meeting.

- Have your markbook as up to date as you can.
- In specific cases have the exercise book at hand.
- Parents may question the number of homeworks you have set. Have a record of these homeworks in your markbook.
- Be polite and keep calm.
- Keep to the prescribed meeting time.
- Never lose your temper or antagonize a situation.
- If you feel the meeting is turning sour and you need help, ask to be excused for a few moments and consult a senior member of staff.
- If your session with the parents merits extra time and they have disclosed information requiring further discussion at greater length, arrange a separate meeting.
- Don't make promises you cannot keep or make predictions that may not come true.
- At the end of the allotted time, politely conclude the meeting and wish them goodbye.

2. At an arranged meeting with parents

- Never see the parents on your own if you feel unhappy about the nature or possible course of the meeting. Consult your head of year or head of department about this.
- Let your line manager know when and where the meeting will take place.

- Don't see the parents in a public place – they may wish to disclose sensitive or very personal information.
- Make the parents feel welcome because they may have had unhappy times when they were at school. They may not be at ease talking to teachers.
- Listen to them and make sure you understand what they are saying. Be patient.
- See the parents on their own first before asking the student to come in to the meeting.
- If the parents have requested the meeting, let them get it off their chest first.
- Have all the necessary paperwork at hand.
- Make brief interview notes.
- Be prepared to reach a compromise in some circumstances.
- If any action plan or definite conclusion is reached at the meeting then read back to the parent the suggested course of action to make sure everyone is clear about what is going to happen.
- Do not let parents have access to other students.
- Do not take sides or make judgements, particularly with parents who are divorced or separated.
- Draw the meeting to a close after the prescribed period of time.
- Well done!

# 4 The Staffroom

Perhaps we should start with a tour of a typical staff-room. Teachers past and present will recognize and identify with many of the things I mention.

Staffrooms to me are never quite big enough. Storage is always a major problem, and because of this they rarely look tidy even after the cleaners have done a grand job at 6am, long before the first tired teaching soul has entered the building. Carrier bags containing bits of costume from a school production four years ago are squashed under tables. Boxes of old textbooks are found in corners of the room, forgotten about and untouched for years. Obsolete computers lie abandoned under rows of lockers. Staffrooms are only thoroughly overhauled, tidied and reorganized when they are about to be redecorated or relocated. Something like this will happen about once a decade, maybe.

There always seems to be a shortage of work areas for staff to mark books, and piles of these exercise books colonize any available table surface. There are easy chairs for us all to briefly collapse into after a morning's slog. However, these pieces of furniture are hardly top-of-the-range DFS and are all too frequently oozing sponge padding and lacking a proper suspension. I remember seeing a regular occupant of one such poorly reinforced seat with his bum about 5cm from the floor and his knees pushed well up above his shoulders. He looked like, and probably was from then on, the incredible rubber man! I worked in one school with a staffroom having an obvious lack of decent chairs. Everyone feared being the last one into the room because they would be forced to sit on what we called the sanichair. It had no seat support whatsoever and you sat on the seat frame looking as though you were using a commode.

Some staff are notoriously untidy, and in my experience it is mainly male staff who are to blame. The worst offenders being male PE teachers. Not only do they leave bits of their kit around the place, which eventually starts to fester and biodegrade, but they also seem completely allergic to washing up their used coffee cups and are guilty of failing to put the rancid remains of apple cores and half-eaten sarnies into the bin.

Sinks in staffrooms rarely look tidy. While the majority of us irrigate our cups after rushing several slurps of coffee at break time, a group of staff will always fail to do so, despite frequent reminder notices placed strategically above the washing-up area. Consequently it is always the sink area with its home-grown penicillin that gives the room its shabby and seedy appearance.

As you gaze around the room, the wall's colour scheme seems obliterated by notices whose appearance seems to take on a collage-like form as we journey through the school year. Notices that should only appear for a week seem to occupy a permanent residency and there comes a time when you really can't be bothered to trawl through the sea of information.

Staffroom noticeboards are usually divided up into labelled sections. There's a zone for the headteacher and their deputies. This part contains news about new appointments, new decisions that have been made and temporary exclusions of pupils (and sometimes staff). It is a very important sector and probably the best kept and presented, for it is usually tended by the head's PA. There's a part of the noticeboard that staff are drawn to like wasps to a jam pot. You will pay homage to this area each day. It's the cover sheet. This is a print-out of the staff who are absent on the day and those whose lessons will need covering by a colleague. The cover sheet has been feared by many over the years. Nobody likes doing a cover lesson. In simple terms it means you surrendering one of your precious non-contact periods and supervising a class for somebody who is sick, late or on a course. Cover legislation has changed over the last couple of years with the introduction of maximum numbers of cover lessons to be undertaken by teaching staff during the year and also the appearance of cover supervisors – education's equivalent of community support officers in the police. In days not too long ago it was teaching staff who did the main volume of cover. But, if the school's budget could stand it, then supply teachers of variable quality would be bought in.

One of my jobs was to organize cover. People who undertook this role were never very popular simply because it was your decision to tuck somebody up with some extra teaching or supervision. You'd walk into the staffroom at about 8.15am and witness the sighs and expletives as a result of your dastardly work. It was the same too when you simply entered the staffroom for a conversation with a colleague. The person would avoid eye contact with you on your approach. You could almost hear their thoughts – 'this bloke is about to snatch my only free period of the day!' I can only describe it as though I had dog poo on my shoe. The cover allocation job was, indeed, the poisoned chalice. However, I feel I must bring to your attention at this point some instances of staff absence requiring cover. I am certain you will encounter parallel examples throughout your teaching days.

# The Staffroom

Doing cover for many years gives you a good insight into the way people tick. Some staff would notch up unbelievable absences. I worked with one bloke who was a marathon walker in his spare time. He'd often boast that he'd walked 50 miles over the weekend thanks to the fitness programme some Scandinavian professor had designed for him. The fact was that he had more days off than Father Christmas. He was always going down with either a viral infection or a groin strain.

There was another colleague who taught maths. Perhaps 'taught maths' is the wrong way of describing the delivery of his lessons. He was a bit too physical with the kids, to say the least. I was once the member of staff on call and was summoned to one of his lessons where I found a pupil fending off this gentleman with a chair. Apparently he'd been up to his usual tricks of antagonizing the youngsters by using rather offensive sarcasm to such a degree that this particular pupil had popped and stood up to him. A brawl ensued, culminating in the liontamer/lion scene I witnessed on entering the room. Both staff and students alike gave him the nickname 'Rocky' because of his bouts of pugilism with kids.

Rocky's unprofessional classroom conduct was accompanied by a poor attendance record involving many hours of lesson cover by his colleagues. I remember asking him how he was one Monday after a week's absence. He was in the process of describing to me some colonic malfunction when I noticed many flecks of white paint on the lenses of his spectacles. I happened to mention my suspicions to a member of the maths department who confirmed Rocky's emulsioning of the hall and stairs in Ponders End.

One of the most memorable gotchas was with an Australian colleague who seemed to be working through the illnesses found in Black's Medical Dictionary. He telephoned in one Friday morning hoping to leave a message on the answerphone. He seemed rather surprised when at 7.30am I picked up the receiver. 'Oh, Brian, it's you,' he said. 'I'm just phoning to say that I won't be in today, the doctor thinks I've got a serious chest infection.' It was then that he realized he should be coughing and proceeded to empty half of his windpipe down the line. All the time he was talking and generating phlegm I was aware of a strange squeaking noise in the background. I thought it must be line interference of some kind. He had just finished explaining the serious nature of his respiratory debility when you could say he shot himself in the foot, or scored the biggest own goal ever. A loud tannoy announcement suddenly joined our conversation. It was 'P & O Stena wish to announce that the 07.45 crossing to Calais is now boarding.' Get out of that one, dingo! The phone fell silent. The curious background noise that had accompanied our conversation was, of course, seagulls. Needless to say we had words on the following Monday.

# The Staffroom

During the period of time I spent doing cover for absent colleagues I came across a group of staff whom I'd refer to as Third Day Resurrectionists. They were staff who would telephone in sick and claim they were so incapacitated by some pernicious illness that they barely had enough energy to lift the receiver. They were unsure about the date of their return, if at all. They would, however, miraculously recover and return to school on the third day to avoid having to produce the mandatory medical certificate. Hallelujah!

A close friend of mine worked at a school in the east end of London. He told me of one of his teaching colleagues who was on long-term sick-leave due to some back problem. Sadly for him, his period of sick-leave was prematurely curtailed. It ceased when the wife of his headteacher, who was one of a party of WVS ladies on a four-day coach tour of the Benelux countries, spotted him driving the coach!

Further along the wall in the staffroom would be copies of NAS/UWT, NUT, PAT and ATL notices. Incorporated into this cluster of trades union information you would find a copy of current or impending pay scales. You can often see a grubby patch where some poor soul has been trying to follow with their finger a column of figures to forecast their pension. What a terrifying thought of having to complete 45 years to qualify for a full pension. The bureaucrats who came up with that one really do need to spend some time in schools.

Perhaps they haven't seen the alarming life expectancy statistics for teachers who complete 40 years of teaching. This legislation change would mean that everyone will die in the job and save the TPA (Teachers' Pensions Agency) a lot of money.

During the late 1970s there was much protracted teacher unrest about pay and conditions of service. Industrial action recommended by the main teaching unions eventually secured better and more realistic pay scales and pension benefits for us all. It was a time when teachers appeared united, irrespective of the trade union to which they belonged. Highly charged and determined times, indeed!

There was a chap in a school where I worked who refused to join a union. He also refused to work to rule. Feelings were so strong about total commitment to the cause that one of the major union representatives, Red Bob, as we called him, drew a chalk mark around the seat where this gentleman would always sit at lunch times. It was a teacher-exclusion zone which no fully paid-up union member must enter. They were deadly serious and pretty emotional times.

I feel it is wise that you become a member of a trade union. They are bodies who negotiate your pay scales and they are there to give you advice and representation should you ever need it.

Somewhere on a staffroom wall will be a copy of the school timetable. I first started teaching in grammar schools. In these institutions the school timetable was something that did not change from year to year. It was a chart that was found in a glass case in the foyer. It was a template that showed lessons and rooms and as staff left, their names were simply erased and the new teacher substituted. The mechanism remained the same as it was last year and the year before that, etc. Being able to produce a timetable, particularly in this day and age, is a real talent. I have met some highly skilled timetablers who spend long hours producing a final blueprint that will meet the needs of the national curriculum, sixth-form courses, staff/student ratios and availability of rooms. However, it is something more than a chart showing classes and rooms. It has power. A timetable can affect learning. It can affect morale. It can even control movement around the school.

I have also worked with some not-so-good time-tablers. One such individual was a deputy head who was terrific with the kids. He ruled with a rod of iron and gave tremendous support to his teaching colleagues. Get him involved with a production of the timetable and he was a disaster. He was to the art of timetabling what Nick Leeson was to a calculator. He was totally unaware that his talents did not lie in the world of time-table logistics. On the last day of the summer term, school would finish at 1pm. The timetable would be posted in the staffroom at 1.15pm by this creative wizard who would then immediately leave school to catch the 4.30pm ferry from Dover. He would be incommunicado (I think that's a small village near Tossa de Mar) for the next six weeks. At the beginning of September he would return to face the flak.

Mistakes do occur, like two classes turning up in the same classroom for a lesson, or sometimes two teachers turning up for the same class. One real corker was a newly appointed deputy, who claimed lots of previous timetable experience, allocating free periods for Year 10 classes. He also timetabled Year 11 classes with science three times during one day with the same teacher. The head should have seen trouble coming when the chap was finding it challenging timetabling Years 12 and 13. For readers who are not timetable literate, these two years go on a timetable first!

A form tutor on the first day of the new school year would have to dictate the timetable to their form. Form tutors will know, it's best to have a good look at it before this task is undertaken. The timetable often needs plenty of deciphering and decoding before it can make sense to a 12 year old, or even a 42 year old. A little bit of forethought in giving a cipher or name to classes wouldn't go amiss. Before national curriculum years, in secondary education we went from first year to fifth year. One particular unprepared fourth-year form tutor was explaining the timetable to her rather noisy class. She had said, over the background din, that 4Q would be doing PE with them at the same time.

'Who did you say is doing PE at the same time as us Miss?' enquired a confused girl. 'Oh for God's sake!' shouted the exasperated teacher, '4Q! 4Q! 4Q!'

'Well, there's no need to use language like that!' replied the girl.

Computers in staffrooms are now common sights. We have come a long way from the days of the ZX Spectrum and the locoscript of the early Amstrads. Teachers are now free to use this sophisticated technology to prepare worksheets, use statement banks for school reports or book their half-term Ryanair flights on the Internet.

Staffrooms are there for staff to relax at break and lunchtimes. They are also places where marking and administrative tasks can be undertaken. New teachers beware! Be careful where you sit in this room on your first day at the school. Teachers tend to be creatures of habit in terms of their staffroom usage. In the majority of cases they sit in the same place before school starts, at morning break and at lunchtime. Sit on one such reserved seat at your peril! You won't instantly discover you have committed a cardinal sin, this will slowly occur to you by the way you are spoken to by the now-homeless member of staff. There is, indeed, a feeling of territorial identity associated with staffroom furniture. One selfish specimen I worked with in a school in Romford would leave a huge pile of textbooks on his seat each time he went off to teach. His behaviour was in the same league as our Teutonic neighbours leaving their beach towels on sun loungers at a poolside in Benidorm.

Staffrooms can sometimes double as a venue for staff meetings. These sessions are essential for dissemination of information and for matters requiring debate. If these gatherings are after school the last thing staff want, having just completed a full day's teaching, is a meeting where some member of the leadership group uses jargon about some new initiative that he/she wishes to implement. The purpose of such a meeting is, of course, to inform you of the fact that you will soon have more work to do and how good this will look on that senior member of staff's CV (though they don't tell you that one). Meetings that arise because of pressure on the senior management by the rest of the staff are usually worth staying behind for. It's a sign that 'There's trouble at t'mill Mr Hardcastle, you'd better come quick!'

Verbosity is common in these get-togethers. What could easily be achieved in half an hour of directed time takes an hour. I would gaze around the room at the tired faces and then guess who would become comatose first. At one school you could always lay odds on it being an ageing head of music, Herbert Gridley. He specialized in violin tuition and the kids called him Fiddly Gridley. When he used to slip into the Land of Nod his snoring was quite audible and he would dribble. One memorable, acutely boring meeting, he dropped off and rested his head on the shoulder of a female NQT who'd just started in his department. Needless to say, he offered to pay for the dry cleaning of her jacket at the end of the meeting.

Meetings in many schools are not confined to after-school sessions. Many places have pre-school meetings on a particular day of the week. They occur about 15 minutes before morning registration. These sessions are designed to bring to your notice any recent issues that require your knowledge and attention and also to remind you to consult the noticeboard about Year-specific pastoral matters. Always make sure you survey this information board for stop-press news, particularly information about students.

It always amuses me when staff walk into these sessions late, having completely forgotten about them. They are very often engaged in loud conversation with a colleague who has also forgotten and everyone stops, looks up at them and thinks about how much of a pilchard they must feel.

The kids are oblivious to these meetings and knock on the staffroom door to ask for a teacher with the determination of a council rent man. It also shows that the person supposed to be on duty at that time to stop them doing this is still swigging a cup of tea in the science labs.

## To summarize:

1. When you are new to the school, ask about un-written laws of the staffroom, e.g. storing books in someone's territory or sitting in some fossil's seat.
2. Make sure you follow the written laws of the staff-room, e.g. washing up your cup or leaving the sink area tidy.
3. Read the noticeboard and focus on information that requires your immediate attention.
4. Ensure you scrutinize the Year noticeboards that should be kept up to date by pastoral staff so that you are aware of essential information about parti-cular students you may teach.
5. Always make sure you know about the fire rules and be aware of your role in any fire drill or evacuation of the building.
6. If you place any notices on this information board, do not leave them there until the end of time. Take down out-of-date notices.
7. Always check the cover sheet and note which class you are covering and for which member of staff. Ask the head of department about set work if there is none visible.
8. If you are away from school because of sickness, always set work even if you feel you are a candidate for the Grim Reaper.

9. If you are on a course and you know you have lessons to be covered, always set work in good time and leave clear instructions about the nature of this work with your head of department.

10. Avoid sellotaping this work to your desk for two reasons:
    - some enterprising student may decide to remove the lot before the teacher gets there.
    - some harassed and absent-minded teacher may peel off all of your day's set work and unintentionally take it with him at the end of the cover lesson.

11. If you have to decipher the timetable for students in your tutor group at the start of the academic year, make sure you understand it before trying to help them.

12. Arrive at school in good time. It's impossible to rush straight into your tutor group with your raincoat on and look in control. You need some time to organize yourself.

13. If you are punctual for the start of your lessons then there's less chance of trouble in the corridors and you've more hope of keeping to your lesson plan.

14. I would recommend you join one of the teaching trade unions. They negotiate your pay, conditions of service, give you sound advice and will often represent you if you experience a major difficulty with some aspect of the job.

15. Try to get down to the staffroom as often as possible so that you can meet your colleagues. You can share problems and often learn from each other, as well as relaxing and drinking that much-deserved cuppa.

# 5 School Assemblies

About thirty years ago, an ageing deputy head passed on to me some advice about doing a school assembly. This information was to be used in times of crisis. Examples of such moments of panic would include if you've either forgotten you were down for it, or your speaker is ill or stuck in traffic. 'Give 'em a prayer and a bollocking. That should fill in the time!' He then proceeded to deliver the slowest version of 'The Lord's Prayer' I've ever heard. This was then followed by an unbelievable verbal assault on the whole school about litter. I know I should have chosen to forget the brief training he gave me but I am sad to say that on rare occasions I too have been a worshipper and a bollocker, but delivered it so well and convincingly that my audience were none the wiser.

As schools have increased in student population, the nature of the school assembly has changed. Schools used to be able to fit all of their numbers into an assembly hall and the school would meet on a daily basis for a corporate act of worship. Nowadays, very few establishments can boast an area that can support such huge numbers. This has led to the assembly now taking place in sports halls, canteens, drama studios, gyms and classrooms. In fact, anywhere that loosely meets the requirements of the DfES.

There's also an assembly programme for the year which is usually put together by the RS (religious studies) coordinator and Year heads. If you are neither of these, or if you are not a member of the Leadership Group, then you will probably resent having to attend assemblies, and also loathe being asked to deliver one. There is, however, the occasional member of staff who is an exhibitionist or an aspiring Pericles who will readily volunteer for such an event. Crackers!

You will witness many assemblies during your career. You will observe both your colleagues and also outside-speakers perform. You will witness top-quality presentations, and also ones that are so appalling you will cry out for morphine to ease your pain.

When you are eventually approached to undertake either a full-school assembly or lead a smaller year congregation I would suggest you do not leave its preparation to the last minute. You will be on show in front of a large group of people and your credibility with your audience is on the line. Failing to give this task some prior thought is about as sensible as someone giving Robert the Bruce a feather-duster for his cave.

The reluctance of some staff to prepare fully can be seen when they deliver a minuscule piece of oratory which is then followed by a long musical interlude. These staff usually preface this song with an anaemic plea of 'I'd really like you to listen to the full meaning of the words in this song.' To me, this is a cop-out and as cheap as the prayer and the bollocking. If you do decide to use music or some visual technology to support your presentation, I would advise you to check it out and make sure it works before you go live. Some schools enlist the help of youngsters who are given such grand titles as the 'technical support group' or 'stage crew'. This bunch are supposed to give you assistance in these matters. My own experience of such motley gangs is that they are often composed of a curious mix of eccentrics and misfits with a dubious range of technical expertise. Some think semiquavers are half-eaten crisps, while others think a musical cue is what you'd do at HMV.

If it's a Year assembly it may well be that your tutor group should feature. I would avoid using a cast the size of *Ben-Hur*'s simply because the more children you employ, the more chance there is of mistakes. It is also more difficult to control and direct. Some kids like to show off and play to the gallery. I would also refrain from giving your tutor group a free ticket to do what they want. They need supervision and some structure to avoid it turning into a romp. I am reminded of the W. C. Fields recommendation that your act should not include children or animals.

Kids also need to be reminded to project their voices, otherwise your weeks of preparation will be lost in ten minutes of patchy audibility. The acoustics of some rooms are atrocious, particularly if you have to compete with the shrieks of laughter from adjacent kitchen staff as one of them informs the rest how her chef of a husband puts holes in his doughnuts.

If you need a microphone then use one. I would, however, be careful of radio microphones. It's sometimes easy to forget that you are wearing one. A colleague of mine did such a thing. He was rather nervous about his assembly presentation and the stage crew kitted him up with a radio microphone. His assembly was excellent and received the customary sitting ovation from both staff and students. At the end of his presentation the headteacher congratulated him on his efforts before reading out a couple of last-minute notices. My exhausted colleague then disappeared deep into the wings of the stage to visit a WC near the PE department office. He then proceeded to eliminate a long stream of urine which crashed loudly into the waters below. This was accompanied by a huge sigh of relief and a 'Thank God that's over with for another year!', all of which was quite audible to the 650-strong audience. Curse modern technology!

If you are quite nervous about doing an assembly, it's best not to let your obvious anxiety show. Try not to walk up and down or sway from side to side, it distracts your audience. I would also refrain from walking among the students while you are talking; those behind you will not hear you once you pass by. The youngsters would then have to turn around and this causes them to fidget. After all it's an assembly and not an episode of *Trisha*. If you are a shaker, maybe steady your hands on a table or lectern. Hiding behind one of these objects can also conceal the fact that your kneecaps are trembling.

One of the biggest mistakes people make when delivering their message is to use audience participation. Invariably this practice carries with it a penalty of doom. It takes a great deal of skill to handle an audience and the majority of us are not Ken Dodd or Jo Brand. If a speaker does use this technique it is usually a sign of inexperience or naivety in dealing with crowds of kids. Avoid questioning your audience with probing starts like 'Who can tell me . . .?', or 'I want someone here to describe . . .', etc. I worked in a school where the head of RE would often ask young vicars or priests into school to speak at assembly time. They were tremendous exponents of such an atrocious technique. Invariably the questions would unsettle the previously tranquil audience and cause unnecessary overtime for staff in regaining crowd control. This style would always lead to a rapid deterioration of student behaviour and provoke the maverick elements of the audience to yell out inane comments.

One of the worst I witnessed was a talk given by a preacher to a Key Stage 4 assembly (14, 15 and 16 year olds). His message was about the need for us to understand more about people's cultures and religions. He wanted to start his message by showing the group from a Romford council estate the different exotic vegetables consumed by people from different ethnic backgrounds. He held up a yellow courgette and enquired of the bored audience 'Who can tell me what this is?' There was a short silent interval, followed by the exclamation 'A dildo!' It had been offered by a Year 11 recalcitrant. The gathered crowd went wild and the assembly slipped downhill into a sea of unrest.

Other people can spoil your often powerful and thought-provoking efforts. A very moving assembly message can be destroyed when immediately after your meaningful words the head of PE stands up and reads a long list of student names he would like to see after assembly. He was anxious to discover who had mooned to a passing motorist on the way home from a district cup match yesterday afternoon. Your hard work, planning and meticulous attention to detail has now had its impact shattered in seconds. Notices and other proclamations should be inserted at the beginning of assembly time.

On the subject of notices, if you ever have to read them out to your seated flock it is always a good thing to scan through them first. This is wise practice since you are sometimes given messages with the legibility of the handwriting of Rameses. It can be acutely embarrassing trying to decipher this scrawl and present sensible information to your semi-comatose throng. Messages given to you at the last minute can put you in a panic.

It was at the time of the much feared acronym ROSLA (Raising of the School Leaving Age) that I was seated in a morning assembly presided over by an extremely well-spoken female deputy whose teaching pedigree was solely grammar schools. The school was a new comprehensive that was a hybridized grammar and secondary modern. It was a Year 11 assembly (fifth form in old currency) and contained a large nucleus of ROSLA students. The Roedean-educated deputy was reading a notice from a science technician who was asking pupils to bring in some plastic containers to be used by the biology department for pond-dipping sorties. The plea was for large containers. The deputy concluded the notice and she then decided to give her own rather ill-chosen words as a summary of the request:

'Remember, Miss Wallace has got small ones, she really does want big ones!'

Needless to say, the place was in uproar. Even the staff were uncontrollable. She eventually realized the double entendre and proudly continued with her notices.

It was sadly the same lady who was responsible for another semantic blunder later on that year. It was Year 11 boys, and again an assembly time. One of the most unpleasant kids in that year was a young psychopath called Archie Cox. He would have made Martin Bormann seem like a nice guy. The deputy was in the middle of her reading to the disenchanted bunch of males when out of the corner of her eye she noticed young Archie messing around. He was about to stab a screwdriver into the large gluteal cheeks of a boy sat immediately in front of him. To arrest this act of aggravated assault, the deputy stopped her reading and bellowed 'Right, Cox, out! Cox, out!' The formerly semi-anaesthetized bunch, momentarily confused by the loud command were now in hysterics, and their laughter went on and on.

One final misuse of language occurred back in the early 1980s. It was at a time when there was a craze involving two plastic balls on a piece of string. If you flicked them up and down they knocked together and made a continuous clacking sound. Kids of all years would bring them into school and play with them in the classrooms, etc. The noise they made was that of an epileptic metronome and proved quite infuriating. Some youngsters got bored with their natural use and quickly discovered alternative applications. In one school a bunch of inventive 15 year olds were seen on the school field behaving like South American gauchos, throwing these gadgets and ensnaring passing first years. In short, the pastime had to cease. A rather colourless headteacher who had obviously been nagged at by a staff who really knew what was going on in his school, got the job of arresting this annoying and often potentially dangerous play. He really didn't have much of a clue what he was talking about, nor was he familiar with slang terms. He started his admonishment in morning school assembly with the following: 'It has come to my attention that certain pupils have been getting their knockers out in lessons. This has to cease forthwith!' Needless to say, this statement was well received by all, including the staff.

Two fairly common instances I feel I must bring to your attention are fainting and farting in assembly. I will cover loss of consciousness first. You may be doing extremely well and delivering a set of which Demosthenes would be proud. Suddenly a huge thud punctuates your delivery. A pupil has fainted. This will be followed by a localized scene of concern which then attracts the attention of the rest of your congregation. From then on, you've lost it. You may as well read out the menu of the local Chinese takeaway.

Some member of staff who is a highly skilled first-aider will then wade in to resuscitate the poor horizontal student. They will apply all of the skills gleaned from the *Reader's Digest* first-aid postal course they have recently completed. The dazed subject is then carried out of the hall with an accompanying background of sympathy and amusement. Your assembly is now quite moribund to say the least.

It is even more of an occasion when a teacher faints in assembly. I distinctly remember a rather protracted morning slot attended by one young member of staff who had been out on the town the night before. He had become so sodden with alcohol into the early hours of the morning that he had decided not to go home but to walk to school and enter the premises along with the cleaners. He did just this and was discovered lying underneath the rug on the floor of the English department office by a horrified caretaker at 6am. He was anxious to prove his sobriety, despite smelling like the floor of a tap room. He insisted on attending the morning corporate act of worship but was observed to blanche, sway and fall forward to the ground. Unfortunately he also head-butted a rather bewildered 14 year old on his way to earth. Not something to put on your CV.

When someone emits a pocket of wind from their rear parts, this too can provide an arresting quality to your painstakingly prepared assembly. The loud, audible vibration cuts through the silence and immediately wakes everyone up and the laughter follows. It is usual for the culprit to claim it was an accident and the poor old teacher closest to the act has to investigate the explosion. It does mean that the pace and presentation of your piece are both irreparably damaged. It's real bad luck.

I was told of an assembly being led by a totally unflappable teacher. He was half way through his set when a colonic emission sounding like a fierce howl suddenly pierced the air. There was muffled laughter from the body of the hall. The teacher paused and asked, 'A wolf? And so close to London.'

There was a second wave of laughter and when this quickly subsided, he continued with his epilogue.

It is often difficult to find material suitable for use in assemblies. It's good practice to cut out and save articles from newspapers. The Internet is also a good resource. Steal from other practitioners. Comedians do, why not teachers? There are a few books that contain suitable material, though these are often produced by clergy or RS teachers and may not hit the spot for you. I distinctly remember one book with a multitude of short passages that were supposed to be suitable for assemblies. It was the most depressing collection of material I have ever read. Each one was about disasters or some personal tragedy. You wanted to sit on a window ledge in a high-rise building after listening to one of its stories.

If you can deliver something that's slightly different to what the kids usually hear, then you are more likely to grab them and keep their attention. If you do many assemblies in the school year and you want to avoid duplication, then it's wise to date them each time you use them. Log down the year or group who listened to your schtick. This will also avoid delivering the same piece to the same bunch later in the year. If you are ever guilty of repetition, the kids will soon let you know. You will witness muffled unrest and be able to detect an audible 'Ohhh . . . Heard it before!' from the audience. You've then got no chance.

Presentation and awards evenings are part of the job. In many ways they are similar to school assemblies. I was presiding over a Year 11 presentation evening where they were to receive their GCSE certificates. I always bargained on getting through the session in about an hour and a quarter. In that span of time we would read out all the student names, and up on stage they would come. Give them a quick handshake and then off they go back to their seats. Meaningful message from me. Job done!

This particular evening did not go as smoothly as I had anticipated. This was due to that collection of repro-bates who called themselves the stage crew. They had been asked to construct a small stage in the hall, made from large blocks. It was an easy task and one that had been done many times before. I was unaware that there had been some lack of bonhomie within the group which led to vital tasks being left incomplete. In short, they had failed to bolt these blocks together and these units were slowly working their way apart. The constant vibrations of two hundred kids tramping across them produced an expanding cavity near the table. After reading the last list of names I obediently leapt up onto the podium to conclude proceedings and dream of a doner kebab on the way home. The leap was fine. As a matter of fact it was a great leap. The landing, however, was not as successful. I crashed straight through the rostrum only to reappear 30 seconds later with an ankle the size and colour of a watermelon, and a suit torn in several places. My nose was bleeding and my spectacles lay somewhere at the bottom of the crevasse. Being a true professional I emerged from the chasm and announced: 'I do apologize about that ladies and gentlemen, it is just a stage I'm going through.'

The evening concluded with sympathy from the parents and comments like 'Nice one sir!' from the kids. I was upset and angry with the fact that a bunch of technical mutants had nearly killed me. I was also peeved that I missed out on my kebab.

The school assembly hall is an extremely versatile space capable of hosting concerts, parents' consultation evenings, plays and even badminton. It often doubles as a dining area. It was at a concert given by our school orchestra and choir that I had to deal with an intruder.

The orchestra had just delivered its own unique rendition of Glenn Miller's 'Pennsylvania 65000' when out of the corner of my eye I noticed a huge figure stood several rows behind me. I looked round and there he was. He resembled images of the sasquatch I had seen on a myths and mysteries programme on television. He had hair everywhere. In fact, he was the most hirsute male I have ever seen. He must have had to comb his wrists. The enormous fellow stood there swigging a can of Tennent's Extra. The chap was doing no harm but was rather spooking the audience. As the senior member of staff at the musical evening, people were slowly looking my way expecting me to deal with the gentleman.

I rose from my seat and slowly approached the yeti-like figure. I was scared stiff and terrified as to how he may react. I stood alongside him and his glazed eyes looked at me and my terrified eyes looked at him. We remained there for a few seconds staring at each other. My heart was working overtime and I was conscious that I was slowly losing bowel control. They do say that immediately prior to one's impending demise you relive your life as flashbacks in a matter of seconds. I had just got up to when I won the knobbly knees competition at Pontins in 1985, when suddenly . . . the band struck up with an ironic loud few bars of the theme from *Rocky*. The sound was unexpected. The distressed head of music had decided the show must go on and had instructed the band to continue with the next piece on the programme. It was a decision similar to that taken by the ill-fated chamber ensemble on the *Titanic*. The sudden blast of brass lifted me off the ground. Fortunately, it had the same effect on Robinson Crusoe in front of me. I emitted the expletive of 'Bloody hell fire!' This remark fortunately proved to be inaudible to the voyeurs. The next thing I remembered was the equally startled Neolith dropping to the ground like a sack of potatoes. He had passed out. God does exist. He remained there, turning strange colours as the resident first-aider did her job. She was an attractive lady too, who sadly did not administer the kiss of life to me. Shortly after, the ambulance came to remove the sozzled, stuporous intruder. At the end of the concert a parent came up to me and remarked, 'I don't know what you said to him, but it certainly had an effect!' I nodded politely and decided not to enlighten him about my real brush with death.

My final example of what can go wrong at a public meeting is when a headteacher was giving a talk to a prospective Year 7 group of parents. It was a very humid and rather sultry evening in Islington. The doors of the large school assembly hall had all been opened to allow any passing current of air the opportunity to bring into the hall the valuable oxygen needed by the audience and speakers. Harold was not the greatest of public speakers at the best of times, and on this particular evening he wasn't exactly cutting the mustard with the potential clientele. He always made a reluctant and uninspiring attempt at demagogy. A parent once informed me she thought he needed a rocket up his arse. They don't mess about, people from Hackney. We were approaching the final phase of the propaganda when suddenly a half-crazed dog bounded into the assembly hall in search of love. Sadly, there was no female dog on the premises to assist. The obvious thing to be loved was the nearest person who was standing. Sadly for Harold, it was he.

The large Alsatian, with its mouth dribbling saliva and its tongue flapping from side to side, made a beeline for Harold's frail form. The parents gasped as the huge canine leapt upon Harold and proceeded to attempt coitus from behind. It took two deputies and the head of Year 7 some time to remove the amorous beast from Harold's body. The highly charged animal was eventually ushered out of the hall only to reattempt satisfaction, this time with the caretaker's leg.

I had to admire Harold. Though slightly shocked by the attempted coupling, he concluded his speech with gusto and eloquence. Perhaps the parent's recommendation was correct, but it wasn't a rocket!

## To summarize:

1. Don't leave your preparation until the last minute.
2. Arrange your OHP, PowerPoint, sound system in good time, and test it before assembly begins.
3. Time your assembly and make sure it doesn't overrun.
4. Use the resource material available to research your assemblies. There are books containing ready-made assemblies. Use the Internet. Poach ideas from colleagues.
5. Don't give your tutor group a free rein. Oversee its preparation and rehearse.
6. Don't be over-ambitious in terms of cast size. Many students prefer behind-the-scenes roles.
7. Try to give your audience something different from what they always seem to hear.
8. Do not offend religious sensitivities.
9. Don't walk up and down or sway from side to side, it distracts your audience.
10. Do not speak off the cuff. You may waffle or dry up. Write out your assembly presentation and double-space it so that you can read it without appearing to read it. Make prompt notes.
11. Don't try audience participation.
12. Use a microphone if you need one.
13. Look at your audience and try to appear dignified, not casual, in your stance.

14. Don't try to be too clever, familiar or matey. Avoid using near-the-mark language.
15. Try not to um and er or to use frequent terms such as 'You know what I mean?'
16. If you are a shaker, hang onto something such as a lectern or table.
17. Keep your assembly and date when you used it last. You can recycle the good ones in years to come.
18. Feel really good about yourself when the kids say 'Ace assembly this morning, Sir. Wicked!'

# 6 School Trips

At the age of 52 I made the conscious decision not to organize or be roped in to supervise any more school trips. Recent legislation from the DfES, together with a determination not to drop dead in the job, forced me to take that decision. I have always said that if you ever organize and lead a school trip then you will need a holiday yourself after it.

The principal directive today is to ensure you have fully researched the trip and that you have completed all of the risk assessments associated with the venture. You must be like Caesar's wife and beyond reproach when it comes to the trip's raison d'être, planning, organization, staffing and safety. You have to pay attention to *every* detail. You must look at what could go wrong and have a strategy in place to avoid catastrophe and tragedy. You must understand that the term 'in loco parentis' does not mean parents are often train drivers, but that it means you are now assuming the role of responsible parent on that trip and will take full responsibility for the protection and safety of their youngsters. Quite a degree of accountability to fall on anyone's shoulders.

One of the most common types of school trip is the day out of school. It may be something as seemingly inert as a trip to a museum or exhibition. Invariably it involves booking a coach as the means of transport. It sounds a simple task, but you may find that the coach arrives late, throwing your schedule completely. In some instances the coach fails to arrive at all and when you eventually get in contact with the coach company proprietor he/she informs you that they have no record at all of the transaction. It is, therefore, always wise to check with the company on a few occasions after making the initial booking. Get it in writing.

Another common problem is that when the coach arrives it doesn't have enough seats. Don't be fobbed off with irresponsible advice such as 'It'll be all right if we use three to a seat'. It isn't all right. Nor is it OK if the vehicle that arrives to take you to your destination is belching smoke and the driver finds difficulty in selecting a gear. If the coach looks as though it was used at the relief of Ladysmith and has not a seatbelt in sight, then don't use it.

Some people may say that I'm too cautious about many things. It's just that over the years, I have witnessed colleagues get themselves into trouble by being rather too casual about coach journeys. A good example is that I always check the coach before the students board. I check it for litter and seat damage. A colleague of mine was accused by a rather unscrupulous driver that one of his party was responsible for ripping the upholstery of a seat. My colleague was convinced that the damage had happened some trips before. The seat was also occupied by the best-behaved and meekest boy in the school. He would have made Aled Jones look like a chav. The driver was adamant and reported the matter to his company. The school had to cough up the money.

Supervision of the students on the bus is an important task. I have seen staff all seated at the front of the coach next to the driver as though they were embarking on a charabanc jolly with the blue-rinse brigade. If you cannot have full view of the kids then you are asking for trouble. Position staff at the back of the coach, then in the middle, and finally it may be worth sticking one at the front to answer any questions the driver may have. Remember, if you do not place the correct number of staff on the bus it's as foolish as Wells Fargo having no one to ride shotgun through bandit country. Placing a member of staff at the back of the coach will also prevent the school receiving complaints from motorists claiming they were given repeated two-fingered gestures or that they were given the full moon treatment.

It's always wise to ask the coaches to arrive before the students. If the school car park is congested with tearful parents then there's nowhere to park the coach and everyone has to walk miles down the road to get on. I have known coach drivers arrive at the school uncertain as to the destination of the trip. This can be most unnerving and not inspire you with confidence, particularly if it's a trip abroad. You either get a driver with whom it is a pleasure to travel, or you are given the most miserable and bad-tempered human in the country. Some are downright paedophobes and should never be allowed on school trips. They start shouting at the kids and are surly with the staff before a coach wheel has turned. I suppose I can understand their tetchy and aggressive behaviour because many have to drive unsupervised masses to and from school. One school I know will now only permit the use of single-decker buses. This is because they were getting so many complaints from the public about being showered with tomatoes and spit from the invisible mob on the upper deck. It's also best to check for litter as soon as you reach journey's end, and pass round a litter sack. This avoids any potential disagreements with the driver.

I am indebted to the journalist Brian Hanrahan for a quote he used in 1982 as he stood on an aircraft carrier during the Falklands war. He said 'I counted them all out and I counted them all back.' He was referring to the jet aircraft which were taking off for combat missions and he hoped would subsequently return. I feel this is the procedure that must underpin any trip, whether it's down the road or to distant lands. Count every student before you depart and count them again before you return. This may seem rather obvious to many, but I can assure you that the success of many a trip has been blighted by a lack of such a fundamental exercise.

It seems wise to give an example here. A little over 20 years ago, three neighbouring schools decided to organize a skiing trip to the Swiss Alps. They had to pool the number of students because the trip was extremely expensive. The trip was only viable if all three schools participated and furnished the required number of students. The organizer of the trip, who was personally responsible for ten students from his own school, was a rather loud and vulgar PE teacher. His claim to being fit to look after the students on the trip was that he could ski, knew first aid and that his second subject was geography. I've always wondered why PE teachers never offer physics or chemistry as a second subject?

The trip took place and it was only on the aeroplane returning to Blighty that one pupil enquired, 'Where's Lee Beaney?'

Young Lee was in fact fast asleep under his bed in an hotel bedroom in Zermatt. He had consumed a surfeit of schnapps the night before and had crawled under his bunk in an intoxicated manoeuvre. Our innumerate skiing consultant, PE teacher and part-time geographer had committed the cardinal sin of not using his fingers to count the pupils onto the coach. Perhaps he only had nine fingers? I needn't elaborate on the consequences of leaving an unconscious student in a foreign land. Suffice it to say that Lee Beaney was eventually repatriated and reunited with his parents. The teacher faced many questions from the head and governors, one being 'When do you want to leave this school?'

Lee Beaney was a fully paid-up member of the ancient order of 'Studentus Problematica'. This group of pupils are those whose behaviour is always in question. They are the potential problems for the school trip. Most teachers who organize school trips don't want to take members of this order but are forced to take them either on financial, humanitarian or equal-opportunities grounds. If we didn't have to take these students along with us, the trips would be easier to manage and supervise. Even a simple visit to the school playing fields can create problems if these challenging pupils are included. Schools in inner cities often have to bus their students out of the area, to use soccer or hockey pitches in more open spaces. One such acolyte of this venerable group of students, a Year 9 lad called Mehmet, consumed a full bottle of Glenfiddich in the short half-hour drive to Cheshunt. The pole-axed Mehmet was then rushed by ambulance to the nearest A & E where he was stomach-pumped and fed charcoal for the next couple of hours. He eventually recovered and continued to be a pain for the rest of his school career.

Alcohol and students do not mix. It is important to remember that if one of your party naively suggests that we should let them have one small drink before bedtime, this is asking for trouble. Many parents would not be happy with such a suggestion, and also some knave or embryo-knave will abuse such leniency. Spending a complete night watching over an inebriated adolescent and making sure they don't choke on their own vomit, or anyone else's vomit, is no fun. Drinking laws abroad do not help. It is easy for youngsters to smuggle bottles of grog into their rooms, which can lead to nocturnal binges and subsequent trouble. A youngster on a school trip to the south of France had to be rushed to hospital at 2am when she consumed half a bottle of Calvados. She was a talented trampolinist who decided to get a bit of late-night practice on her bed. She overlooked the fact that her bed was underneath the revolving fan. She is now an asymmetrical trampolinist since the fan removed three quarters of her ear.

Your supervision roster should ensure that you know where the students are and what they are doing. The pre-trip meeting with students and their parents allows you to highlight your behaviour requirements. If parents and student both sign the code of conduct information sheet then you have made things totally clear to both parties. If they don't sign, then the student does not go.

Many teachers who organize school trips have said that the staff accompanying the children are more difficult to deal with than the pupils themselves. It is often the case that some school trips come about because they sound great in the planning stage, but when the nuts and bolts of staffing the trip come about it is difficult to find suitable people. You must have people who are trustworthy and reliable. Do not take staff as mere passengers. Should you ask them to undertake a supervision at a certain time then they have to be there. When school trips are abroad, just as alcohol is a problem with students it can also be a concern with colleagues. A junior member of a history department failed to return to the hotel one evening to assist with a lights-out duty, having 'copped off' with a local senorita in Barcelona. I am sure he was proud of the consummate Anglo–Catalan relationship, but his colleagues were most unimpressed. They were the ones who had to cover his duties and also spend some time down the police station filing him as a missing person. In short, don't get desperate and recruit just anyone. Plan your staffing before the trip goes public.

It's also easy to overlook basic safety information for the children on school trips abroad. Simple things like telling the students that when crossing a road on the

Continent you don't look right, then left, then right again. You do the opposite. I heard of some poor Year 9 student eager to parler français who was knocked down on the promenade at Boulogne having just stepped off the ferry. She was taken to hospital accompanied by a member of staff who stayed with her until her parents arrived many, many hours later.

A former colleague of mine told me of a school trip to Paris that was not only ill-fated at the start but also continued to give bad vibes from Dover to the Arc de Triomphe. The coach arrived with the relief driver thinking the trip was to Brussels. The crossing to Calais was interrupted several times by the ship's purser demanding to see the teacher in charge of the St Jude's party. The kids were re-enacting *Mutiny on The Bounty* and terrorizing the passengers. The hotel in the Clichy area of Paris was right next to a brothel, which entertained both students and staff. The *bateau mouche* trip along the Seine had to be cancelled because of strong winds . . . and also the fact that the teacher in charge had lost the group ticket. Three students got completely stoned on skunk on the last night. One of the lead teachers had a blazing row with the other co-leader and stormed off to her bed at 8pm, refusing to take any further part in the holiday. 'Holiday' is precisely what these trips are not. A search of the students was undertaken before catching the return ferry home.

You could get away with that 30 years ago. It revealed more flick knives than were possessed by the Mafia. One student even had a 12-inch bush knife stuffed under his pullover and down his trousers. I think he was relieved to have it confiscated since he later told his mates that it was nearly circumcising him.

Some students sign up for school trips abroad not really knowing which part of the world they are to visit. They want to go because it will be a bit of a giggle with their mates and also to have some freedom from their parents. One student I knew thought Pisa was in Spain, whilst another thought the Balkans were islands at war in the south Atlantic. Another budding Alan Whicker was prevented just in time from changing his money for a trip down the Rhine into drachmas rather than Deutschmarks.

Passports are another nightmare. There's always one who arrives at the school at 5am without one. They manage to leave it on the telephone table and Mum has to imitate Ralph Schumacher by going home to retrieve it. Once we travelled from Heathrow to Barcelona and in the party were twins. They amazingly sailed through two sets of passport control with each other's passport. Easily done you may think with twins, but the twins were boy and girl. Watch out for staff too, they can often forget documentation. I arranged a fishing trip to Ireland and despite numerous reminders my teacher co-driver forgot his driving licence.

'I've got my passport though,' he said, expecting me to heap praise on him. Of course, you don't need a passport for Ireland.

Stress the need for E111 forms. It's amazing that some parents haven't heard of these. One lady from Dalston thought they were something to do with food additives.

A neighbouring school wanted to organize a football trip to the United States so that their successful Year 10 team could show their trans-Atlantic counterparts how good they were. Two young members of staff took charge of the organization. They were unwisely left to their own devices and made all of the arrangements without some experienced senior colleague oversee-ing their progress. The trip was agreed at a governors' meeting and the parents duly coughed up an amazing amount of money to finance the venture. On arriving in the States not a football was kicked because the insur-ance our two inexperienced colleagues had arranged was done on the cheap and did not qualify any of the party to undertake sports that could lead to physical injury. OK if you're taking a bridge team but not if you are down to play six games of soccer. The dynamic duo returned to face the flak. Not something to include on your CV.

Collecting money for school trips can be a real pain. Payment cards, similar to those used by credit com-panies for families paying for something on the drip, are essential records of payment. These cards are signed by school and parent on each instalment. A former colleague, who always seemed to be organizing school trips, would walk around the school with so many of these cards in his pockets he looked like the council rent man. My advice is do not, if at all possible, accept cash. There will also be administrative problems if the cheque paid for the trip does not bear the same surname as the student. Decide on an acceptable amount of spending money that parents should allow their children. Do not allow the kids to have all of the week's money at the start of the holiday because there will always be some that blow all of their pocket money in the first few hours.

Rules concerning students not entering the rooms of students of the opposite sex need to be made clear for obvious reasons, and it is the duty of your supervisory team to ensure this does not happen. I don't think I've been on one trip without someone in the party failing to uphold this rule. On one trip it was a male member of staff entering a female colleague's room for some considerable time. How I knew of this, you guessed it . . . the kids told me!

It is sensible to take a first-aid kit and sick bags for the journey. Ensure you have all medical details of students and that they have their medication with them. It can be a veritable nightmare if an insulin-dependent diabetic student loses their insulins and you have to replace them when you are in a remote village in Umbria.

An example of the need for a tour party leader to always know about what his/her students are up to during a school trip abroad was recounted to me by a former colleague. He was leading a trip to Provence. The coach could not park adjacent to the hotel and so instead would drop the kids at the bottom of the lane, leaving the party a short walk to the hotel. Each day the group would pass the property of a local resident who kept a rather mangy-looking dog behind a fence in her garden. The sad-looking dog did I suppose bring out the James Herriot instinct in the children and also in one canine-devotee member of staff. It was the last evening of the tour and the group had finished their evening meal. Several pupils plus the Crufts enthusiast had left the dining room early. Approximately half an hour later there was an almighty bout of hysteria in the foyer of the hotel. The old lady who owned the dog was shouting and screaming at the proprietor of the hotel. She was inconsolable and seemed furious about something that had happened to her animal. The owner of the hotel was trying to translate for the leader of the party what exactly had happened. He initially thought the students had either set the dog free or poisoned the creature. What had in fact happened was that the small group of dog sympathizers had decided to smuggle some food out of the restaurant and feed the beast. They were lobbing bread rolls and bits of pâté over the fence in an attempt to improve the animal's diet and put some flesh on him. At last the hotelier managed to glean the actual reason for her hysteria and anger. The dog was in fact a champion truffle hunter who had to be kept on a restricted diet so that it could give of its best at the impending truffle-hunting championships next week. The dog was now bloated with cream cakes and pasta and really couldn't give a damn if it never sniffed a truffle again. Irreparable damage had been done. The mutt was now deemed not fit to even sniff a lamp post. Provençal–Essex relationships soured from that moment. The touring party was booed out of the village and told never to return.

Some parents along with the rest of the general public are becoming increasingly litigious and seem only too ready to apportion blame. I would advise teachers to use external providers such as recognized school-tour operators if they are planning major trips. Certain visits such as day trips to towns, museums and exhibitions may be easier to organize in-house. Risk assessments are now a vital ingredient in the preparation and planning of any trip. Read carefully the good-practice guide issued by DfES on health and safety of pupils on educational visits. Best of luck!

## To summarize:

1. Have a clear reason or purpose for your educational trip, such as theme/adventure/sightseeing.
2. Gain outline permission from the headteacher.
3. Choose a reputable travel company that is ABTA-approved. Recommendations from other schools may be helpful here.
4. Calculate the cost of the trip, plus a reserve to cover extras and emergencies.
5. Obtain consent from the headteacher and governors.
6. Send a letter to parents and include consent form, medical and dietary information section.
7. Keep proper accounts/card receipts. Record dates of payment. Do not accept cash. Watch out for the name on the cheque being different from the student's name. This can throw your accounting.
8. Do a pre-trip inspection tour. Look at issues like security, food, rooms, excursions. Complete all the risk-assessment documentation.
9. Choose reliable staff who will accompany you. Remember, take no passengers!
10. Arrange a meeting with parents. Cover issues such as passports, spending-money, E111, insurance, supervision, pupil behaviour, alcohol, safety, seat-belts on coaches and supervision on ferries.

11. Parents may wish to know about 'free time' for students. Cover meaning of the term 'in loco parentis'.
12. Hold a meeting with the pupils and cover the same issues. Set out rules for rooming, rules of the hotel, boys not allowed in girls' rooms, behaviour on the trip.
13. Get together a medical kit and ensure you have a qualified first aider.
14. Children should bring their own medication.
15. Explain about limits of insurance concerning mobile phones and CD players the students may wish to bring on the trip.
16. Give a list of staff and pupil names to the caretaker and the office staff. Addresses and contact telephone numbers.
17. Telephone the coach company to verify times and schedule.
18. On day of departure ensure the coach and you are there before the pupils. Have some sick bags for the delicate travellers. Don't wait for lates because your job is to get the party to the ferry or airport.
19. You will have established a communication network from student to parent to notify safe arrivals. Mobile phones with students can have their positive uses.
20. Bon voyage, and may your nervous system stay intact!

# 7 Inspectors and Advisers

There are two statements you may hear in your life-time that are classic examples of dubious comment. The first is:

'I can assure you the cheque is in the post.'

The second:

'Good morning, I am an Ofsted inspector and I'm here to help you.'

I'm afraid I cannot change my overall opinion about this double act even after 30-odd years of being perse-cuted by them. To me, and I feel sure that many of my colleagues would support me on this, Ofsted inspec-tors are a form of low-life as yet undiscovered by David Attenborough. Those members of the teaching pro-fession who do not subscribe to this classification are obviously the potential inspectors and advisers of the future. I cannot imagine why teachers decide to turn their backs on their colleagues and then make the decision to terrorize and inflict pain on them. I have my own theory about such a choice. The majority I have met don't look as though they could survive the daily demands of a life in full-time teaching. I have been advised and inspected by many who look as though they have bailed out of the brotherhood simply because they couldn't hack it in the classroom any more. I have also worked with some appalling classroom practitioners who went on to positions of advisory authority and then proceed to tell good, effective classroom teachers how it should be done. I make no unreserved apology about the fact that I actively despise them. George Bernard Shaw would have revised his witticism to 'Those who can, teach. Those who cannot, inspect' were he alive today.

I worked with a female colleague who was an absolute star in the classroom. She had been teaching for nearly 25 years. She was brilliant even with the most challenging of pupils. She worked hard. She prepared her lessons thoroughly. She inspired pupils. We were in the middle of an Ofsted inspection and her lesson was being observed by one of these men in grey suits. It was a really tough group with many unpredictable and unstable kids. The group's name was 11P. The staff who taught them said the letter P stood for Psychopaths. At the end of the lesson the inspector said he would award her a lesson grade 4, which meant it was satisfactory. His reason for only allotting this score was that he had noticed three or four of the students going 'off task' towards the end of the lesson. My talented and by now exhausted friend sharply replied, 'Listen cock. Off task? Off task? Three quarters of this lot are off their bleedin' heads. Never mind off task!'

The ashen-faced important man said nothing. He just picked up his shiny, expensive briefcase and left the room. He left behind him a dejected, despondent and thoroughly demoralized ambassador of the teaching profession.

The school receives notification of its impending inspection in a small brown envelope. Immediately, this causes the head to develop cardiac discomfort, followed by similar changes in blood pressure in his senior-management group as he makes known to them the contents of the letter. This happy band then decides to inform the rest of the staff at the earliest convenient moment, which usually occurs at an emergency meeting or the first possible scheduled staff meeting. The head will deliver the glad tidings in a super-confident and reassuring way. The message will be dressed with remarks like: 'We all knew we would be in line for an inspection sooner or later.' Or, 'There's no need to worry, I'm seeing the Chief Registered Inspector next week and then we'll have a clearer picture of the nature of the inspection . . .'

None of these pleasantries help the staff since many have lost lower-bowel control on hearing the words 'Ofsted inspection'.

Eventually, the REGI (Reporting Registered Inspector) speaks with the whole of the staff and he/she illuminates the various parts of the inspection. They always add the caveat that no member of staff should worry unduly about the inspection. . . . You can cut through the tension hovering above the staff as they listen to the apocryphal tidings. Statements like 'You have nothing to fear from an inspection' mean they have very little insight into people management. Every person in that hall will now lose sleep, go off their food, drink more Côtes du Rhône and be unbearable to live with for the next few weeks. Staff will learn that adrenaline is brown.

In a rather strange way they are right, we shouldn't fear an inspection. After all, the people observing and reporting on us are human, aren't they? Don't answer that if you've just had a bad inspection. Next time you are inspected I want you to imagine the bloke with the clipboard standing in front of you, not in a suit, but in his underpants and socks. Imagine them being sick after eating a dodgy burger, or having their haemorrhoids dressed. It may help.

A close friend of mine currently works in the sump of Essex. In this part of the county they struggle to recruit teachers. His school has been given the nickname Fort Apache. It's that lively. Residents of the area adjacent to the school have to be careful when closing their windows for fear of trapping the hands of young offenders.

The school was recently given a full Ofsted inspection and my friend was observed delivering a lesson to a difficult Year 10 class. He was criticized by the inspector (about 15 years younger than him and someone who'd been out of the classroom for heaven knows how long) for the lesson not having a distinguishable middle. My friend said wearily, 'Well, I'm sorry about that. What are you going to do? Sack me?' The apprentice stormtrooper, not sensing that he may have upset the only graduate chemist working in that dreadful part of the planet, reaffirmed his organization's requirements that all lessons should have a start, a middle and an end. These people can be paid £500 a day for that complex information. It's always a surprise to me how they can come up with such an analysis even when they leave your lesson before the end.

I remember having one of my sixth-form lessons observed by a strange-looking character who wore a visiting Ofsted inspector's badge. He had large, protruding incisor teeth. His complexion was grey. His suit was obviously purchased from an Al Capone tribute shop. He looked as though he'd just been exhumed.

He left my lesson about three quarters of the way through.

'Yes, that was good,' he said. 'But I noticed you asked everyone a question except those two girls on the second bench. You should involve everyone,' he sagaciously concluded.

'Erm, but there's 15 minutes of the lesson still remaining. How do you know I wasn't planning to ask them questions then?' I replied irritably.

'Oh, just an observation, just an observation,' responded the man who'd clearly undergone surgery for a charisma bypass.

That's just it you see. They always feel they have to point out something to you. Something you can act on or bear in mind. They will not listen to your side of the story. They will remain intransigent. If you disagree with their opinion, then that's just tough. This reminds me of the old wisecrack: This Ofsted inspector went for a heart-transplant operation but they had to cancel it because they couldn't find a stone big enough.

I can cite yet another example of inspectors feeling the need to criticize perfection. A head of maths who was held in high esteem by the school and its students was observed by a rather young Ofsted commandant. The lesson was a top-band high-flying maths set being coached to secure A* at GCSE in Year 10. They would then go on to sit additional maths in Year 11. The group contained about 20 students who were all distinguished mathematicians. The lesson fulfilled all of the criteria and could not have been improved. The *Obergruppenfuhrer* of an inspector said he could not give the teacher an 'excellent' because there was no differentiation built into the lesson. The maths teacher replied, 'But they are all aiming for A* grades, they are all very talented mathematicians! How can I possibly inject elements of differentiation here?'

'Well, nobody is ever awarded excellent. There's always something that can be improved,' replied the SS man.

I don't care what some teachers say about not minding the fact that visitors are in their lessons. The bottom line is that nobody wants their classroom practice put under the microscope. Having inspectors or advisers in your lesson makes you paranoid. You may be in mid-verbal flow and think you are doing well and then suddenly out of the corner of your eye you will see them write something down! At this point you automatically think you've done something wrong. What can it be? You were doing so well. Actions like these can throw you slightly. At the end of the lesson they may not be able to give you instant feedback and you are left to sweat for several hours until a verdict is given. My advice, should they ever try to engage you in conversation, is to tell them nothing other than your name, rank and DfES serial number.

I have seen exceptional teachers reduced to trembling heaps of cytoplasm during inspection week. Hypertension, delirium tremens and induced conditions like these are uncalled for. No hard-working and conscientious teacher needs to be put through this mangle.

In an attempt to make things easier, the inspectors used to tell you the classes they would like to see. It may well be that they choose the worst class you teach. It may be the class that you live in fear of during the school week. Now that is real bad luck. They will often ask staff to give them a resumé of the nature of the class and an outline of your lesson. It is a great temptation to write that this class is internationally recognized as being the mangiest herd of reprobates ever. You feel you must inform the inspector of this before the lesson begins so that he/she will empathize with your daunting task. I feel that would be a waste of time, since it is now a recognized fact that all Ofsted inspectors have the area of their brain that deals with understanding, compassion and humility removed as soon as they get their stripes. Instead, you should write something less specific and as benign as, 'They are a challenging group.'

Remember, your lesson should contain elements of those three famous solicitors Pace, Rigour and Challenge. A former colleague of mine once described his inspected lesson as having plenty of pace, since the kids were chasing around the room. There was also plenty of challenge as an unpleasant and threatening kid offered him out during that period four. The rigour of the lesson metamorphosed into rigor mortis.

If you are fortunate enough to be informed of an impending lesson inspection it may prove helpful if you inform the pupils. Many of them respond positively to blackmail and bribery. It's often worthwhile telling them that the inspector is coming into the lesson to see them rather than you. This of course has an element of truth in it, though at the time it's hard to convince yourself of this fact.

The students may really want to help you out. One delightful Year 7 group told me to give them the questions I'd be asking them beforehand so that they knew all the answers and would impress this Oftel inspector, as they called him.

It is also advisable to write up on the board your lesson aims and objectives at the start of the lesson. It's amazing how many kids then scratch their heads and wonder from where this technique has suddenly appeared. I would also recommend that you don't choose this lesson to experiment with new things. Don't try to be too cocky and suddenly try roleplay with kids when you've never done it before. Stick to a 'safe' lesson.

I recall an inspection many years ago in the age of hymnbooks. Students were supposed to possess their own hymnbook as part of their school uniform. Sadly as the students moved through the school years, so their choral desires waned along with the number of hymnbooks brought to assembly. During this particular inspection, the whole team of HMI (Her Majesty's Inspector of Schools) descended on the Monday morning assembly. They dotted themselves around the hall to gain maximum experience of the way morning corporate worship took place. The kids played an absolute blinder for the school because from the stage you could see hymnbooks being passed to groups of students clustered close to the attending inspectors. It really looked most convincing that every student had a book and was singing. Hallelujah brothers and sisters! A great start to the week.

The complete reverse can happen when kids can land you in it. I had only been teaching about three years and the school was being inspected by HMI. Because the Queen was associated with this lot I never really liked her from 1974 onwards. A special science course had been developed by some wise people designed to attend to all the needs of ROSLA students. It was called the LAMP project, an acronym that stood for least academically motivated pupils. But, you mustn't tell them that.

One of the topics we were to cover with this array of malcontents was a unit on flight. Other modules bore inspiring titles such as paints and dyes!

I had about 26 students when they were all there, which fortunately for me wasn't very often. The task in hand was to construct their own balsa-wood aeroplane and get it to fly. Technical details such as assessing drag and stall potential were a tad too heavy for the group.

An HMI closely resembling Humpty Dumpty entered the room. His appearance defined the term 'endomorph' and he looked like a walking ellipse. He introduced himself to me and he shook my trembling hand. He asked me what the group was doing and said, 'Well I'll just wander round and ask the pupils a few questions.' The group weren't too bad at that moment, it was period one and the majority hadn't really woken up. Some were still part drunk or hungover from the night before and the rest, even though fully awake, looked as though there was little electrical activity in their bodies.

The HMI went over to a lad whose upper body was slumped over the bench. His head was resting on his arms and he was half asleep. The young man was called Alfie Daws. Alfie, amongst other odd traits, had a penchant for putting cats into dustbins and setting fire to them. Even his close mates found this behaviour disturbing. The egg-shaped inspector sat down next to him and quietly asked him why he was not actively constructing his aircraft. Alfie did not move, but spoke out in his very deep and characteristic monotone, 'I took mine home last night and tried to fly it in me bedroom,' he said.

'Oh, good!' replied the egg man. 'And what happened then?' he persisted.

'Well,' droned Alfie, 'It went round and round, and round and round then straight through the fuckin' window!'

The HMI noticeably twitched as the expletive was uttered. 'Now leave me alone!' moaned Alfie. The HMI did in fact leave him alone. I thought my teaching days as a young 24 year old were over. I could see my P45 being posted already. A career selling double glazing looked ominous.

The inspector finished his tour of the group and curiously enough seemed satisfied with the fact that they were all occupied. He did say to me, however, 'That chap at the back seems a little sorry for himself. I should give him another task if I were you.' I nodded in agreement. Much to my relief he started to leave the room. But just as I thought the ordeal was over a lone voice bellowed out from the ranks, 'Who was that fat geezer?'

It happened just as the inspector was about to close the door. To my huge relief the door closed, and stayed closed.

The reader will detect my serious jaundice concerning the inspection process and those individuals charged with responsibility for conducting this procedure. However, inspections and the inspectors will never disappear. There has to be accountability and quality control by an outside agency even though schools today are way down the road of self-evaluation. So we must expect input from people who are responsible for implementing this inspection. All of us must shoulder their scrutiny and analysis of our teaching and management. I would suggest you deal with this by understanding what they will look for in your lessons.

## To summarize:

1. Do you show good knowledge of the subject you are teaching?
2. Do you translate and present this knowledge to pupils in such a way that they understand the subject matter?
3. Do you show effective classroom control?
4. Do you involve all the students, irrespective of their ability?
5. Do you set the students tasks that explore their knowledge and understanding?
6. Does your lesson show differentiation?
7. Do you encourage students to overcome their difficulties?
8. Do you use homework effectively to reinforce what has been learned during the school day?
9. Do you use resource material effectively to complement and support your lesson?
10. Do you assess pupils' work? Do you mark their books and tests according to departmental policy?
11. Do you keep records of attendance and performance?
12. Do you plan your lessons?
13. Does your lesson show the necessary pace, rigour and challenge?
14. Does your lesson have a recognizable start, middle and end?

15. Does your lesson start with the students knowing what are the lesson's aims and objectives?

If you can give a resounding yes to all of the above then you have nothing to fear. You will be awarded a Very Good. If you maintain all of these qualities in every lesson of your teaching life you should then consider becoming a member of our future inspection teams.

# 8 You're a Tutor as Well

When you chose to enter teaching as a career, your principal wish was to teach your specialist subject. It also is a great help if you happen to like kids. You may be a geographer, but when you begin your first teaching post you should be mindful of the fact that you take on the whole job package. Undoubtedly you will be given a teaching timetable relating to the geography curriculum of the school, but you will also become a form tutor. This role should be just as important to you as ensuring your students know all about landscape features caused by glacial erosion, and the socioeconomic implications of gold-mining in Kalgoorlie.

As a tutor you are a key player in the pastoral infrastructure of the school. I have heard many ways of describing the impact of the form tutor in a school. They are usually engineering terms such as you are the cornerstone, keystone or linchpin of the pastoral framework of a school. You are someone who will play a vital role in both the academic and personal development of the students in your charge.

Many people view the tutor's job as being one of the hardest of all in teaching because it is one for which you receive very little training. Like all pastoral jobs it's hard to quantify your day. You never know what a student in your tutor group will tell you about problems at home, difficulties with work, problems with fellow teaching colleagues or issues with their peers. Your mission as a tutor is to make the transition of a student from Years 7 to 13 as smooth as possible in terms of their academic success, career potential and their personal and social development.

The pastoral organization in schools should ensure that no tutor ever works in isolation. You must never feel as though you are on your own. Tutors work as part of a team led by a pastoral manager such as the head of year or head of house. These people in turn have their work overseen by a senior line manager. You should always be able to receive support and guidance from any of part of this team. The mechanism is, and should be, the same as in the academic camps of the school. These two pillars of the school are not detached from each other. The pastoral system should underpin and work in tandem with the departmental or faculty structure of any school.

When you are allocated a tutor group it may well be a completely new start for you both. You may be a Year 7 or a Year 12 tutor and you will be responsible for this fresh bunch of youngsters who have never existed before as this new unit. However, as happens in many schools you will find yourself in front of a seasoned crew who may have been together for the last four years and they could have had a range of different tutors before you. Taking on a tutor group part of the way through a year is also a more challenging prospect. One of the initial things you have to deal with is that your predecessor may have done things differently to you. So, if you meet your tutor group for the first time and they are lying across the desks listening to their iPods, purchasing cigarettes from the class tobacconist and generally ignoring you, then you will have a rather uphill task on your hands.

Your head of year should have spent some time briefing you about your new flock, though sadly sometimes this may not happen. If at all possible, read the files of the students in your charge. In the days of paper filing systems you would always be drawn first to the fattest files, usually symptomatic of students with ongoing and protracted problems. It is also your responsibility to ensure that each of your student records is constantly updated so that if a pupil transfers to another school or if a suspension appeal hearing takes place, the information about that student is both accurate and up to date.

If this is not the case then you will place the senior member of staff representing the school in a difficult and often humiliating position.

Getting to know your students also implies you are aware of any special needs of the students in your charge. You must know your students with learning difficulties, your dyslexics, your EBD students, your English as a second language students and also your gifted and talented youngsters.

Your pastoral middle manager will tell you that you are to act as the first point of communication between home and school. Parents will telephone you in the first instance, rather than contacting the head of year. It is wise, therefore, to make sure you know the family circumstances of each student in your tutor group. There is nothing more distressing for a parent who has lost their spouse to receive a hastily written note from you addressed to Mr and Mrs. Similarly in cases of divorce or separation of parents you should know whether it's Mum, Dad or both who need to be contacted. If there is any need to contact home it is always best to check with the head of year/house first, in case there has been any change in domestic arrangements about which you are unaware, or if it is wise to address the issue in this way.

If you receive any communications from home about bullying, a recent bereavement or sickness in the family you must inform your year head. I recall one memorable

letter received from a parent asking me to relay important information which read, 'Wallace's undescending
testicle suddenly appeared at the weekend. I would be
grateful if you could inform Mrs Appleby (HoY) and
Mrs Crosby (School Nurse).' She was particularly anxious
to know if it did.

'PS. Please tell Mr Donaghue (Head of PE) that Wallace
can now do the high jump.'

You may also have to work in association with your
pastoral Year supervisor in opening up lines of communication with other teachers and the support services.
It is essential to remember that you will have greatest
contact with the 25 or more students in your charge
during the working week. You will register them twice
a day, have times with them when other Year groups
are in assembly and also have timetabled sessions for
personal, social, health and citizenship education
(PSHCE). In short, you are the teacher who is expected
to know a great deal about every individual in your
tutor group. It is fortunate that gone are the times of
Tom Brown's schooldays when the tutor did nothing
more than call the morning and afternoon attendance
register, make disparaging remarks about the pupils
and box their ears.

You must talk to your students and gain their trust,
because very soon they are going to be asking you for
some help or guidance. Create time to listen to individuals in your group. If you can't see them at that

particular moment, then create some space during that day. It may be an urgent matter. You may be the only adult with whom they feel they can speak. Be a good listener. However, I must throw in a few words of caution here. If a student wishes to make a disclosure to you and asks you not to tell anyone, you must point out to them that depending on the nature of what they say to you, you may have to involve other people to help with the issue. Examples here would be those relating to child abuse. Your school will have a policy in place for matters concerning child protection, and this should be rigidly upheld. If you are unclear about issues like this then discuss it with your head of year. *Never* keep important matters to yourself, you must share them with your pastoral line manager.

Pupils will tell you many things that will highlight much about themselves, their social lives and their lives at home. Such dialogue helps you to understand them more as individuals and not just as students at your school. It helps you complete the tapestry of their young lives so far. Some offer this information readily and will often make you laugh about things that have happened to them. I distinctly remember one member of my tutor group telling me that his dad could fully clothe me in terms of suits, jackets, shirts and trousers for the meagre sum of twenty sovs. I had tuned in to *Crimewatch* the week before and hastily declined the offer.

Some youngsters are rather less forthcoming with information about themselves or their families, and you must respect their wishes. Don't probe too deeply. The essential thing is that you have credibility with the members of your tutor group. Don't say things you don't mean and don't make them promises you can't keep. If you say you are going to do something, then do it. If you let them down you will lose their respect and forfeit their trust in you.

Keeping an accurate attendance register of your group, however, is still an essential prerequisite of the job. Not only is this procedure necessary for legal reasons; the attendance register is used in compiling school statistics and also of importance in writing references for employment. Poor student attendance and punctuality is your job to monitor. Make sure you are familiar with the school's policy on attendance. Electronic registers of today are supposed to make the whole system of attendance checking less complicated. Students who arrive for morning registration and then vanish like Lord Lucan should be far easier to detect.

Looking for patterns in attendances can also bring to the surface areas for concern. It may be that young Lee Tattersall in your tutor group seems allergic to maths lessons on Friday mornings, or that Tanya Gilby has suffered from 'flu and then miraculously recovered each Tuesday for the last four weeks! In association with accurate recording of attendance you will have to receive and check letters from home regarding absences, hospital or dental visits. You will receive explanatory notes such as, 'Chris was not at school yesterday because he went to the hospital for his eyes.'

Some letters you receive will relate to the curriculum. One such classic I encountered was, 'Please tell Mrs Deakin it is true that Yolanda's textiles homework was eaten by our dog, Rex. She does not seem to believe her so tell her that she can come and have a look at his sick in the garden if she wants proof!'

You may have days when there is much to do in the short space of tutor time. There may be a sack of correspondence that you must wade through. Nevertheless, always scrutinize the notes and don't just mark them as ready for filing by someone in the office. It is your duty to check for any forgeries or bogus notes. You should be able to recognize counterfeit signatures and fraudulent explanations. One student I knew spent hours practising his dad's signature, which I had to admit was a truly accurate representation. The only trouble was that the calligraphy of the rest of the letter looked as if it had been penned by Blind Pugh.

Some teachers have a pathological fear of doing Year or school assemblies. You may well be one of these souls. Part of your duties as a form tutor is to lead your form in producing a tutor-group assembly. This task may fall upon you about once a year. Good advice is not to leave the organization of this performance until the last minute. Ask for some ideas about assembly themes from your tutees well in advance. It's always best to have a few ideas yourself and cleverly steer your group in that direction. If this is done in a subtle way they tend to believe it was their suggestion in the first place. Assemblies on smoking and drugs have been done to death and can be platforms for certain members of the group to show off to their friends. You must stay in control and any poor taste or insulting per-formances will reflect on you. Never underestimate the talents of members of the group. You will hear some mature and impressive ideas from them. Similarly, you may find that you have some aspiring Kate Winslet or Anthony Hopkins waiting in the wings. Structure it well, but avoid a cast-size equivalent of *Dr Zhivago*. Each member of your group can have some input and role in its implementation. (See Chapter 5 for more on how to prepare for assemblies.)

If your school has a dress or uniform code then it is up to you to ensure that members of the tutor group uphold such recommendations. They should leave your morning and afternoon registration sessions fully dressed. Jewellery checks should regularly feature at registration times. I remember one Year 9 student, Everton St Jean, who frequently attempted to wear more bling than Mr T of the A-Team. Each morning we would go through the ritual of de-chaining him. He really seemed quite grateful for this therapy since the metal was bringing him out in a verdigris rash and its weight giving him a stiff neck.

Uniform is just one aspect of a school's regulations. Your job is to ensure that the school's ethos and rules are supported on a daily basis. You may not always agree with some of its values and stipulations. You may not, for example, concur with the fact that girls have no summer uniform and are subjected to the laws of heat physics in their black blazers, skirts and black tights on hot days in July. You should not undermine the school's doctrines in front of the students. They should be able to engage the leadership team on issues like this through school council.

Another administrative chore for you as the tutor is to ensure that homework planners, diaries or organizers are being correctly completed and that parents have signed them. This task, though rather time-consuming, can give you plenty of information as to the amount of homework that is or is not being set by your teaching colleagues. It is a laborious yet essential task. Don't wait for parents to pick you up about lack of or too much homework being set. Try to pre-empt their intervention and head off these concerns at the pass, as Big John Wayne would say. Again, check signatures in the book are authentic. Some students could forge a Rembrandt!

It may well be the school's decision that each tutor implements the tutorial programme. You may be part of a specialist team responsible for teaching some aspect of PSHCE about which at least you have some knowledge. Alternatively, you may teach in a school where this programme is in disarray – possibly due to high levels of staff turnover. You find yourself teaching about industry, profits and prices, a subject alien to you since your degree was in medical physics. If you don't take these lessons seriously and prepare for them in the way you would prepare for one of your subject lessons, then the students will respond in a negative way. Fortunately, the majority of schools today have a well-coordinated programme under the guidance of heads of year and staff with a paid responsibility for PSHCE. The material covered in it from year to year should complement the personal development of the students. Always insist on resource material being available to you well in advance. Material given to you at the last minute means a poorly prepared lesson. You must never be expected to go it alone and feel you have no support in this area.

One increasingly important role for you as a tutor is to be responsible for monitoring the academic progress of the pupils in your group. You are often referred to as the 'learning tutor'. You have a key role in academic review days when you can openly discuss the progress of the student with their parents. Again, it is essential that you receive all subject information in good time so that you can give purposeful and helpful analysis

125

and guidance to both student and parent. Producing written summative reports about student progress is also part of your brief. These will embrace comments on personal development and success outside the classroom.

You may set up interviews and see parents of students in your tutor group on your own if your pastoral line manager is confident the agenda is within your capabilities. If you are apprehensive about this then ask for their presence. If for some reason you are unable to attend a parent interview chaired by the head of year, make sure you provide any background notes or information to assist your colleague.

Some parent interviews may require much skill and experience, particularly those covering contentious or sensitive matters. You should leave these to more experienced and senior members of your pastoral team. You will develop your professional skills and expertise by asking to sit in on these meetings. I am reminded of one such parent interview many years ago about a boy in my tutor group who was always in trouble with teaching staff. My head of year asked the parents to attend a crisis meeting about young Hamish's continued poor behaviour and chain of exclusions. I sat in on the meeting and listened to the very professional way my Year head was conducting the session. The parent was a rather corpulent chap called Mr Mann. He had a daughter in Year 7 called Isla, named after where she had been conceived. Mr Mann was a commissionaire at the local cinema and would proudly wear his uniform 24 hours a day. Staff reckoned he had commissionaire pyjamas too!

He sat there in the meeting looking like Horatio Nelson and I could tell he was becoming more and more distressed listening to the catalogue of his son's misdemeanours. He suddenly snapped. He shot up and pointed to me and shouted, 'Right, I've heard enough! Get the bleeder in here!'

I dutifully cooperated with his pugnacious request and brought the boy into the office. 'When I get home you little git, I'll bleedin' well strangle your parrot!' he shouted at mega volume. The boy became hysterical and was inconsolable. Underneath Hamish's tough and recalcitrant exterior there lay a genteel and passionate predilection for parrots. After almost 30 minutes of negotiations and arbitration Mr Mann finally agreed not to commit avian assassination if Hamish's behaviour improved. Miraculously, the boy's conduct did change for the better and his feathered companion survived. What an unexpected result!

Meetings are often unwelcome additions to your full working week. Pastoral team meetings or individual sessions with your pastoral manager are essential parts of the termly calendar. It is important that information concerning the Year group and tutor groups be disseminated in both directions. It is also an opportunity to discuss issues common to all tutor groups in that Year. You are, remember, part of a team and the effectiveness of that team hinges on productive and useful communication.

Most schools today will organize in-house courses that allow you to broaden your professional skills. Some of the twilight sessions may have a pastoral focus. I would encourage you to take advantage of such sessions. They may range from learning what ADS (attention deficit syndrome) is all about and how it impacts on you, the teacher, to topics such as developing counselling skills. They are run to help you become a more complete teacher.

I undertook a course on bereavement counselling and found that it equipped me to understand the possible ways youngsters grieve when they have lost someone near and dear to them. It made me aware that the same grieving processes can take place when families are split by divorce or separation.

The mother of a young girl in my tutor group died after a short period of illness. Even though I prepared our tutor group and her teachers for the girl's eventual return to school, the girl remained quiet and uncommunicative with her peers and adults for a long period of time. She refused to discuss her loss with anyone, even her dad, sister and bereavement counsellor. The course I had attended enabled me to understand the many different ways people can show their grief and loss, and this was just one example.

It was just over six months after her mum died that I found a piece of paper in the back of her homework diary. The words written on the paper have stayed in my mind for over 20 years and still bring a lump in my throat. It read, 'My Dad did not go to work that day. He came into me and my sister's room and I knew something was wrong. He was shaky and he began to cry. He said, "Your Mummy has gone to heaven and the angels will look after her." Me and my sister cried and cried. I miss my Mum all the time and my Dad does too. When I think of her I cannot hold back my tears.' The girl had made a start in communicating about her loss in the long grieving process.

To organize tutor group activities and teams may sound like an easy task when your Year head mentions these duties to you at the beginning of the academic year. However, in your attempt to develop a sense of tutor group identity and corporate spirit you may be faced with a wave of apathy from a considerable number in the group. This is particularly the case when your predecessor had the get up and go of Rip Van Winkle. Nevertheless, it's down to you. You must fight this inertia and put across to them that all of them can participate in representing the tutor group in some way. Some of the group will be doers, some organizers and some background workers. Everyone has a contribution to make. Sports-day team organization is a perennial problem, particularly if you are unfortunate enough to have acquired the most corpulent and anaemic proportion of students in the Year. In this case I feel you are quite justified in asking for arm wrestling and origami to appear on the sports-day menu.

Pastoral middle managers are often viewed as the engine room of a school. They really allow the school to tick on a daily basis. They are very busy people and that is why they rely heavily on your cooperation and hard work with the tutor group. They will expect you to maintain discipline of your group. Don't leave it all to the Year head or head of house. You have a role to play too. The students in your tutor group are your responsibility, and if they do wrong you will be expected to pursue this matter with them.

Establishing a rapport with a tutor group comes more easily to some than others. Most tutors take pride in the responsibility of watching young people develop through their secondary-school years. They are upset when their pupils let themselves down. They are thrilled when the youngsters succeed. Forging a good relationship with a tutor group is one of the most rewarding things in teaching. They may send you a birthday card, offer to clean your car and maybe even give you a present at Christmas.

I was a Year 8 tutor and my group gave me a selection of Christmas presents on the last day of term. One of the group was a rather lively character called Wayne Beardall. His parents owned an off-licence not far from the school. He brought in a large cardboard box and placed it on my desk.

'Merry Christmas, sir! This is from me, my Mum and Dad', he said.

The box was slowly leaking a watery substance. Thinking about off-licence and gift, I automatically suspected alcohol! I put my hands in the leakage and tasted the liquid.

'Is it Boddingtons, Wayne?' I enquired.

'No sir,' came the reply.

I tasted the exudate once more.

'Is it Tetley?' I persisted.

'No sir,' said Wayne.

I now licked my fingers with greater determination.

'Is it Whitbread then, Wayne?' was my final question.

'No sir, it's a kitten!' chuckled Wayne excitedly.

Happy Christmas.

### To summarize:

1. You act as the first point of contact between home and school.

2. You are the person who is expected to know the most about your students.
3. You should have good listening skills.
4. You should be a credible figure with your flock, and someone they can trust.
5. You are their learning tutor and monitor their academic progress.
6. You need to regularly check homework planners.
7. You are to keep an accurate attendance register and follow up attendance and punctuality issues.
8. You are responsible for upholding the dress or uniform code of the school.
9. You have a role to play in implementing the citizenship and personal development programme in the school.
10. You are to maintain accurate and up-to-date records of personal information about your tutees.
11. You should assist in contacting parents, should the need arise, and attend parent interviews.
12. You should attend pastoral team meetings.
13. You should maintain discipline at form-tutor level.
14. You should be prepared to organize a tutor group assembly, teams and activities.

## 9 Keeping on Top of Your Job

I was conducting a mock interview with a most pleasant ITT student who was about to embark on attempting to secure a permanent teaching post. We had reached the stage of the interview when I asked him about his strengths and weaknesses. He gave an impressive account of his strengths, but in his response to my question on weaknesses he then proceeded to pour out his heart and soul all over my desk, worthy of a sacrificial act perpetrated by the Ancient Aztecs.

'I feel I don't work too well under pressure', was his first career-ending reply.

'I tend to get a bit lazy when I've got lots of work to do', was his second attempt at hara-kiri.

I felt like stopping the interview there and then. However, I decided to wait and reveal my horror at the end of the simulation.

## The SAS Guide to Teaching

Teaching is a stressful occupation that make tremendous demands on your time, both at work and at home. Today, much is spoken about the value and skills of time management. It is absolutely right for us as teachers to explore this concept since over the years we have had progressively more and more demands placed upon us. You must be able to strike the difficult balance between doing all that is expected of you as a classroom teacher, and having a quality home life too. At certain times of the academic year this equilibrium is impossible to achieve. Pressures from marking examination scripts and completing reports are just two examples of matters that impact on your hours at home.

One of the fundamental pieces of advice on time management I can offer to teachers starting their careers is first to buy a decent watch, and then follow this with a purchase of an alarm clock that is both reliable and simple to set.

The watch is to a classroom teacher what a fine-tooth comb is to a nit nurse. You simply cannot function without one. Your meticulously planned lessons often hinge on moving from one activity to another so that the session has a prescribed start, middle and end. If your classroom hasn't a clock and you don't possess a watch then you are clearly in the *merde* as the bell suddenly goes to mark the close of your lesson, which is now only three quarters complete. The watch is also a helpful artefact for someone who is teaching a challenging class.

It can bring you joy when you glance down to find that there are only five more minutes of the lesson remaining. It can, however, be the device that triggers palpitations and sweat as you discover there are still 45 minutes to go!

If you are someone who finds it difficult to rise in the morning, then it is essential you read on. Poor time-keeping for the start of morning school, in particular, seriously impacts on your colleagues and the pupils in your charge. You create more work for the person arranging cover, the teacher delegated to supervise your tutor group, and you also set a poor example to the members of this group.

I recall a young teacher who frequently found it diffi-cult to escape from the arms of Morpheus and would arrive full of excuses such as problems with his car's big end, to him suffering from 'the runs' (problems with his big end?). He was a nuisance and a liability. After several episodes of these dramatic entrances at the beginning of period one, a deputy head resembling Boadicea took him aside and said, 'Listen Justin, if I can get my family up, three kids breakfasted and off to school and still get to work on time, I'm sure you can do a simple thing like switch off your alarm clock, crawl out of bed and bloody well get yourself off to work!' Justin did heed her advice and his punctuality did improve. She was absolutely right to do this. It is imperative that your timekeeping be beyond reproach.

This does not only apply to the start of the day but also to the lessons you teach.

If there is one thing about the job that I do not miss, it is marking. I find it incomprehensible that teachers can volunteer for marking SATs or other public-examination scripts on top of their routine quota of school marking. Marking is a dominant part of your teaching life. It must be done so that you can assess the progress of the students you teach; it highlights difficulties they may be experiencing. Schools today have marking and assessment policies and it is essential that your marking should be in accordance with these criteria. It will be acutely embarrassing for both you and your head of department if during any inspection of books it is discovered that you are going your own sweet way.

Some young teachers make the fatal mistake of setting frequent homeworks that involve detailed marking. Such work does need to be set but make sure that it is not too much of a demand on you each time you take in their books. It is wise to set a variety of work that can be assessed in different ways. Some exercises will involve teacher tick and flick. Some work can be marked in class by the students themselves. Homeworks can take on many different forms that don't always need marking, such as research or learning homeworks. Remember, you have many classes who will all be making demands on your free time. Some pre-planning for the half-term ahead will enable you to put together a structure for marking that will be paced and not create too many crisis points. Your teacher planner is the diary for recording such arrangements.

When you do undertake detailed marking, avoid overdosing on red ink. I have seen some marked work that shows more red than a student's bank statement. It must be disheartening and demoralizing for any pupil to be returned such work. Marking needs to be done in a sensitive and positive way, as well as being critical. Set the student reasonable and achievable targets for the next piece of work. If a piece of work is extremely below par then see the student on an individual basis, out of earshot of his/her friends.

You may also be tempted to take home too much work that needs marking. Be realistic with yourself and gauge exactly how much you will be able to mark in one evening or a weekend. Most seasoned campaigners would suggest one pile of books per evening is enough. However, you will see some of your colleagues shovelling stacks of books into their cars. Equally, some staff will be witnessed attempting body-building techniques using carrier bags full of folders and exercise books as they struggle home on the bus. Both practices reflect poor planning, panic, an impending Ofsted inspection or an unrealistic appreciation of the dimension of time.

Always remember to record the work you have marked in the markbook section of your planner. This may seem an obvious suggestion, but I have seen planners with

137

half-empty records even though the painstaking marking process has been accomplished. This will also be of help if parents question the progress of their child. Have it handy at parent/teacher consultation sessions. Return work that has been taken in for marking as quickly as possible. If you fail to do this on a regular basis it demotivates pupils since some of them may have tried very hard with a particular piece of work and they are eager to see how they have performed. If you do not return marked work by return of post then you will also lose credibility with the group. I remember, as a tutor, reading out a notice from a member of staff who had lost her mark book. The reply was from a young lady called Nadia who never took prisoners and had an answer for everything. 'I don't know what all the fuss is about, Sir. She never marks our books anyway!'

'She must have left her lottery tickets in it Nad,' added Nadia's mate, Celise. Celise too was a knowledgeable 16 year old who would frequently top up her permanent fake tan with a damp teabag.

During the course of a school day, many people will tell you many things. Get into a habit of writing things down that need attention. It is impossible to carry this list around in your mind. Get pleasure out of striking through completed tasks. Nothing gives you less kudos with the pupils than promising them something and then forgetting all about this guarantee. Make written notes in your planners of anything in your lesson that went particularly well. It may be a way you explained a difficult concept. It may be an amusing quip that went down really well with the punters. Similarly, note down any pieces of advice given you by your colleagues about tackling certain topics or issues. You will not forget them for next year if you write them down.

The academic year diaries are a must to assist you in your personal organization. Use them in association with your planners. You don't need to be a Samuel Pepys and record every emotion. They just help in planning your term, allowing you to log important dates such as parents' evenings, report deadlines and meetings.

Keep copies of letters you send to parents. Also make sure you keep a record of any telephone conversations you may have with them. File them where they should be filed so that you can lay your hands on them if needed.

You should aim to complete your lesson preparation in good time for the following week. This is particularly essential if you need to order apparatus or resources from your department or outside agency. A science technician on Monday period one will not look upon you too favourably if you present them with a list of apparatus the length of the Bayeux Tapestry required for 9T, period two on that same Monday. Try at least to be one week ahead in your preparation and planning. This is hard, particularly for young teachers starting their teaching lives. There never seem enough hours in the day. It does get easier the more you get on top of your subject. Remember to look at your week. You will have to take on board the days you are on duty, have meetings or are running after-school clubs when you are planning your week.

In your early days in teaching you will have to attend meetings and probably not chair or convene them. It is during this embryonic phase that you soon learn the characteristics of good and bad meetings. You will sit through sessions chaired by a colleague who simply hasn't a clue about organizing productive sessions, and you will think your time could be better employed marking books. You will see meetings attended by hordes of staff. The meeting has a population the size of Italy and you will witness that nothing gets done. You will experience meetings dominated by two or three vociferous staff who don't give the other three a chance. In some meetings, the agenda will suddenly appear at the start of the session, giving no time for prior attention. Some agendas will be too long and have no chance of completion. This is only too apparent when it takes three quarters of an hour to cover minutes of the last meeting. Some agendas have no clear sense of purpose. All of these possibilities will eat into your lunchtime or your time after school. You will learn techniques of how to stay awake and look interested. However, the main learning point from all of this negativity is that you will learn how productive and purposeful meetings *should* be run.

There is often a tendency to over-volunteer for things when you first join the job. You are anxious to show willing and for people to see that you are committed to the profession. You seem to have endless amounts of energy. Be careful! The PE department is always on the lookout for new recruits to take teams, or your own department may ask you to assume responsibility for some chore nobody else will touch. You must pace yourself and remember that your week as it stands is full with teaching commitments, marking and lesson preparation. Don't be afraid to say no to people if you really think their request will add to your time and stress. If you dress this negative with pleasantries, then you will not upset them. If you do want to take the Year 9 soccer team for training after school on Wednesdays and perhaps give up half a day on Saturdays to see them always being annihilated by neighbouring teams, then there is nothing wrong with that wish. However, build that commitment into your weekly planning and allow for the time it will consume.

Teachers are examples of workers who frequently toil through their break times. By the time you have finished packing away at the end of your lesson at morning break, there seems little time to run down to the staff-room or faculty office for a cuppa. Similarly, many staff have reduced lunchtimes because of important things they must do. I would advise you to try to have a lunch break and to socialize with your colleagues. Your nervous and cardiovascular systems need that time to recharge. Building in periods of relaxation into your working week are essential prerequisites for your diary. However, some young members of staff may unwind a little too over-zealously at weekends, and find their Sunday hour of marking goes out of the window along with the whole of work on Monday. Try to get the balance right and explore the many different relaxation techniques or pastimes and not just those which begin with 'Chateau . . .' and end in 'Produit de France'.

## To summarize:

1. Think of the school year in manageable chunks of half terms.
2. Record meetings, parents evenings, report deadlines and exam dates in your academic year diary.
3. Use your planner to chart your week.
4. Order equipment and apparatus in good time.
5. Write things down that need doing during that week, and then cross them off as the tasks are completed.
6. Keep an organized filing system.

7. When you are planning ahead, think about the volume of marking that these lessons or homeworks will incur.

8. Set different kinds of homeworks that avoid rigorous and detailed marking.

9. Return marked work as expeditiously as possible.

10. Set realistic and achievable targets for the student whose work you mark.

11. Marked work should help the student and not damage their confidence and self-esteem.

12. Always mark to the school's marking policy.

13. Do not volunteer for too many things.

14. Be realistic about the amount of work you take home.

15. Try to have a lunch break.

16. Build into your week relaxation times or occasions when you can treat yourself.

17. Learn from your colleagues about ways of coping. Don't be too proud to ask them. After all, we are all experiencing the same stressful situations.

# Index

# Index